The Gospel according to James Baldwin

The Gospel according to James Baldwin

What America's Great Prophet
Can Teach Us about Life, Love, and Identity

Greg Garrett

ORBIS BOOKS
Maryknoll, New York 10545

ORBIS BOOKS
Maryknoll, New York 10545

Founded in 1970, Orbis Books endeavors to publish works that enlighten the mind, nourish the spirit, and challenge the conscience. The publishing arm of the Maryknoll Fathers and Brothers, Orbis seeks to explore the global dimensions of the Christian faith and mission, to invite dialogue with diverse cultures and religious traditions, and to serve the cause of reconciliation and peace. The books published reflect the views of their authors and do not represent the official position of the Maryknoll Society. To learn more about Maryknoll and Orbis Books, please visit our website at www.orbisbooks.com.

Library of Congress Cataloging-in-Publication Data

Names: Greg, Garrett, author.
Title: The gospel according to James Baldwin : what America's great prophet can teach us about life, love, and identity / Garrett Greg.
Description: Maryknoll, New York : Orbis Books, [2023] | Includes bibliographical references. | Summary: "An exploration into the continued relevance of James Baldwin's writings and wisdom"— Provided by publisher.
Identifiers: LCCN 2023007215 (print) | LCCN 2023007216 (ebook) | ISBN 9781626985391 (trade paperback) | ISBN 9781608339969 (epub)
Subjects: LCSH: Baldwin, James, 1924–1987—Criticism and interpretation.
Classification: LCC PS3552.A45 Z675 2023 (print) | LCC PS3552.A45 (ebook) | DDC 813/.54—dc23/eng/20230307
LC record available at https://lccn.loc.gov/2023007215
LC ebook record available at https://lccn.loc.gov/2023007216

For my daughters, Lily and Sophia:

May they live bravely and love deeply

Contents

On Pilgrimage, Seeking St. James.   1

The Life of James Baldwin.   10

Baldwin as Prophet of Humanity   19

Baldwin on Culture   27

Baldwin on Faith.   57

Baldwin on Race   82

Baldwin on Justice 113

Baldwin on Identity 142

Journey's End, New Beginnings. 161

Acknowledgments 167

Notes. 171

On Pilgrimage, Seeking St. James

You gave me a language to dwell in,
a gift so perfect it seems my own invention.

—Toni Morrison,
at the 1987 memorial service for James Baldwin,
Cathedral Church of St. John the Divine, New York City

Why James Baldwin? We might begin here.

It was summer 2019, and despite my real and almost incapacitating fear of heights, I found myself on a bus climbing higher and higher into the Swiss Alps, with a sheer, almost incalculable abyss looming just past my right elbow.

I had come from Paris to Switzerland chasing the writer, critic, and activist James Baldwin, who has become more and more important to me as I have thought, taught, and written about race, film, and reconciliation, and simply about how we live on this Earth.

In his evocative Jamesian fiction, I found myself both transported to exotic worlds and understood in the very space I occupy. In his essays drawn from his own unique experience and observation, I found compelling answers to many of my own questions about racism, history, religion, identity, love, and justice. In his trenchant but thoughtful criticism, I discovered a necessary counterpoint to my own narrow Anglo angle of vision, gained insights I could never have reached through my own straight white middle-class filters, and was inspired to continue arguing that art and culture can and must be read not just critically but also in the light of how they represent, distort, and transform our own lives.

I read the news. A lot of it. Too much, perhaps. I'm active on social media. I speak and write and preach about controversial social and theological issues. So I am well aware of the charged and riven culture in which we live, and that, given the fault lines and the chasms between us, James Baldwin and I might seem to have little to talk about.

We face each other across huge divides, any one of which would seem in the present moment to mean we are unintelligible to each other. He was born Black and poor in Harlem; I was born into the white middle class, and my childhood was suburban, sometimes even rural. I have driven a tractor, ridden a horse, stacked hay bales, for God's sake.

His formal schooling ended after high school, yet he is rightfully revered as one of America's great thinkers; I have an embarrassment of college and graduate degrees and still know I do not know enough.

He officially left the church after early piety; I was a young religious malcontent who became deeply and even traditionally Christian in middle age.

He was a gay man in a time when that identity could have gotten him jailed, wounded, or killed; I am a heterosexual male raised in a homophobic church and culture that extolled Adam and Eve, not Adam and Steve.

In a time when any of these dreadful dichotomies cause people to gather into their own gated communities to slam the barriers shut against those on the other side, James Baldwin and I differ in so many ways that some might rightfully ask why on earth I was seesawing up the side of a mountain in Switzerland, why books by and about Baldwin have weighed down my backpack for years in travels to Paris and Harlem and Washington, DC, and—Jesus God, Greg, please do not look out that window—now to Leukerbad or, as Baldwin knew it, Loèche-les-Bains, Switzerland, where sixty years ago on at least three occasions, Baldwin came to write and talk and drink and make love.

For that matter, how can we explain why so many students at Baylor University, where I have taught for over thirty years, who have read Baldwin with me (some of them, yes, people of color, some of them LGBTQ, but many of them white or straight or conservative Christian) stop me in the hallway months (or contact me years) after our class together and tell me they cannot stop thinking about *The Fire Next Time*, or "Sonny's Blues," or *Go Tell It on the Mountain*, or *The Devil Finds Work*.

How to explain why the white writer Nicholas Buccola, whose *The Fire Is upon Us,* a great 2020 book on the monumental University of Cambridge debate between Baldwin and William F. Buckley, says that "For me, and for many others, Baldwin is the sort of writer who alters your perception of the world and forces you to consider and reconsider your place within it."[1]

How despite these myriad differences, my white Baylor University graduate assistant Daniel Smith thinks Baldwin "the most balanced mind in American letters," an artist who speaks into Daniel's own life and struggles, into all our lives and struggles, in fact, reminding us of "Baldwin's preoccupation with the

ruins of the self and his awareness that all such ruins are connected, if only we would tear down certain walls."[2]

How my friend Ella Prichard, a white, eighty-something
woman from the Deep South with a lot of family history tied
up in race, wrote me that "to my astonishment, I identify with
Baldwin—not as though my experience has been in any way
comparable to his, but because he writes of the era I grew up in.
I recognize the truth in what he writes."[3]

How Black writer, professor, and preacher Michael Eric
Dyson, as a boy in Detroit, found that Baldwin's essays were
"reading me into black manhood with the wise counsel and
steady affection of a big brother or a loving father."[4] How Anglo
Californian seminarian and photographer Bob Fitch read *The
Fire Next Time* as a class assignment in 1965 and immediately
decided "to pursue work as an activist rather than to minister from the pulpit," photographing Martin Luther King and
others during the civil rights era, and spending the next fifty
years using his pictures as a tool for social change.[5] How Suzy
Hansen, who grew up a working-class white girl on the Jersey
Shore, wrote in *The Guardian* that when she encountered Baldwin's work in college she met a teacher "who gave me the sense
of meeting someone who knew me better, and with a far more
sophisticated critical arsenal than I had myself."[6]

These testimonials come from all sorts of people, from all
over, and they could fill their own book. Over the years I have
been working on this project, I have often heard how Baldwin has
lighted the path for someone, no matter how similar or different
their own experience from his. It is a startling urging of commonality from this distinctive literary artist. If our current cultural
Venn diagrams are accurate—and certainly we seem to segregate
ourselves into gated communities in all these ways and others—
then James Baldwin should only speak to Black people. Or gay

people. Or radicals thinking ardently about equality and justice. Or writers and artists. Or people born in the 1920s. Or people who have been in Harlem. Or Paris. Or Turkey. Or Switzerland.

As I write this, I imagine those Venn circles tightening, narrowing, choking the very life out of anyone who isn't, well, James Baldwin.

But when I read Baldwin, when I listen to him speak, when I introduce him to others, the precise opposite seems to take place. What I and readers like my student Daniel feel is expansion, growth, a widening of possibilities. I find myself and my students popping our buttons as we spread in every direction. We experience an enlargement of what it means to be human in Baldwin's presence, gain burgeoning insights into why we might be here, what we are made for, how transcendence feels, what beauty is, how we're meant to live with each other, how we are called to love each other and to be responsible for each other.

My friend Robert P. Jones described this expansion beautifully at the American Book Awards, when he shouted out his gratitude to Mr. Baldwin as he accepted the award for his own fine book, *White Too Long: The Legacy of White Supremacy in American Christianity*:

> It's perhaps surprising that the writing of a black, gay author hailing from Harlem a generation before my time would resonate with me—a white, straight guy who grew up a Southern Baptist on the working-class side of town in Jackson, Mississippi. But from the first time my eyes first danced across the lines his hands first tapped out on a manual typewriter, I had an experience that is best described in a word from our shared Christian faith: "Communion." I felt Baldwin speaking to me, and the power of his writing called for an answer.[7]

It's not that James Baldwin did not have a distinctive human footprint; he most assuredly did. Interviewers sometimes chose to open conversations with him by citing his identity distinctives and asking if they represented a challenge, although Baldwin tended to call them a gift. But as Mr. Faulkner, revered and wrestled with both by Baldwin and myself, once said, every great writer deals with the huge universal themes by writing out of their own tiny little postage stamp of land.

We are who we are because of who we are. And we can speak to the world because of that.

I came to Switzerland—three hours on a high-speed train from Paris, three hours on a local train to the village of Leuk at the base of the Alps, an hour sweating in the hot sun—Switzerland was also caught up in a general European heat wave—for the bus into the Alps, and what turned into the longest forty-five minutes of my life as we climbed and switch-backed and slowed to a crawl to negotiate tight curves and avoid oncoming traffic—and please God, Greg, do not look out that window—because I believe in my heart and in my bones that James Baldwin matters. That he spoke and is still speaking to us. And that anything that might help me better understand his life and his work—even a trip up the side of this mountain, the worst amusement-park ride of all time—was something to be experienced, reflected on, and valued.

I also believed that Mr. Faulkner was right about each artist's individual postage stamp, that although James Baldwin had his own very particular set of human experiences, his writing and his life offer us universal truths. Different as we are, at the end, we are not so different.

Like Baldwin, I have loved and lost, have been laid low by depression and heartbreak, have contemplated stepping off the planet. Like Baldwin, in my life I have been constricted and even damaged by the exercise of religion in my vicinity. Like Baldwin, I have been scarred by the unwanted attentions of a powerful white man who was used to getting anything he wanted. Like Baldwin, I have felt isolated and misunderstood, have felt pushed to the margins because I see the world thoughtfully and try to exercise my art faithfully. And like Baldwin, I have attempted to figure out who it is I actually am, have worked through identities and beliefs, have sought what makes a life worthwhile and a community worth living and dying for.

Every book I have written—it's more than a few now—has ultimately grown out of this desire to understand the world and my own place in it. It's not a thing I ever do lightly, even taking on a new project with as compelling a subject as James Baldwin. As Baldwin knew, writing is often painful, with daily failures that can crush your spirit. Like many writers, I'm committing myself to years of thought and effort and months away from my family, and I have discovered that at heart, like Baldwin, many days I really would just prefer to travel, or to spend time with the people I love, and enjoy good talk and food and drink. Like Baldwin, I want to throw myself head first, soul deep, into loving the person who makes my heart sing, and yet here I am sweating my way up into the Swiss Alps while my bride is fixing our girls breakfast in Austin, Texas.

But also, like Baldwin, I believe that some people do have a special calling, whether because they can see the world a little more clearly, or because they can write about it a little more cleanly, or both. Baldwin had those gifts. He thought of himself as someone called to be a witness, someone who could help all of us understand the world and our place in it better because of what he saw and what he wrote.

Baldwin was, like his stepfather, a preacher in his youth, and he knew the Scriptures as well as the figures in them. He saw himself as a prophetic character like Jeremiah, a person given a special commission to tell the truth, no matter how hard or how painful that might be. Baldwin matters and will always matter because he took that call seriously, because his writing and his life confronted everything we still struggle to figure out.

Maya Angelou spoke at Baldwin's 1987 funeral at the Cathedral of St. John the Divine about one of their conversations: "We discussed courage, human rights, God, and Justice. We talked about Black folks and love, about white folks and fear."[8] James Baldwin speaks directly to many of the things that keep us up at night or exercise us during the day: to racism, to identity, to love and sexuality, to the various kinds of violence human beings do to each other, to faith and meaning, and to the prophetic role of the artist.

Indeed, James Baldwin has been weighing down my backpack, my syllabi, and my heart because this Black gay expatriate writer is and always will be an exquisitely thoughtful guide to What Matters, whether in the Age of Kennedy, the Age of Trump, or the Age of Whatever Comes Next.

I followed James Baldwin up into a remote village in the Alps not because I expected to meet him there—I already meet him daily—but because I believed going on this quest might help me meet myself. That's what great artists do—out of their own experience, through their command of image and language, they hold up a mirror that helps us to see and know ourselves, helps us to learn, to love, to hope. The essay "Stranger in the Village," which Baldwin wrote after his first winter visit to Leukerbad, reminds us that life is unbearable without hope.

On the way up the mountain, I must confess, I did regret my decision to come. But I had faith in Swiss engineering, and at some level deep, deep down below my terror, I did not expect to die on this mountainside. So I fully expected that when I arrived near the mountaintops, I would have the great privilege of seeing what James Baldwin saw, of imagining his experience there, and of learning some things in the process.

But that trip to the mountaintops, that journey far away from my comfort zone, had me wishing for solid ground, for the familiar, and maybe that too is why I came. The Familiar can be the enemy of the True. Baldwin once wrote about one of the things he treasured about his time in the church, how believers were counseled to "do our first works over." What that meant, he offered, was to reexamine everything about your life: "Go back to where you started, or as far back as you can, examine all of it, travel your road again and tell the truth about it. Sing or shout or testify or keep it to yourself: but *know whence you came*."[9]

So that's actually our first stop, not Switzerland. We'll go back as far as we can, we'll start from the beginning, and we'll begin seeking the truth together—with Baldwin.

The Life of James Baldwin

Although I find it hard to imagine a world without him, we have only had a James Baldwin for the past century, and it was some years before he became the artist and activist memorialized in St. John's Cathedral. James Arthur Baldwin was born in 1924 in Harlem, the grandson of a slave, and the eldest of what would ultimately be a family of nine children. He never knew his biological father; his mother, Emma Jones, reportedly left him because he was an addict. Emma married a Baptist preacher, David Baldwin, when James was three.

James always had a strained and painful relationship with the stern, pious, and distant David Baldwin, who treated him with less affection than he did his biological children. They were never close; in the essay "Notes of a Native Son," James recalled that he had never known his stepfather well: "When he was dead I realized that I had hardly ever spoken to him. When he had been dead a long time I began to wish I had."[1] Nonetheless, biographers see this father/son relationship as perhaps the most foundational one in James Baldwin's life.

Susan McWilliams spoke of how Baldwin believed that one of the most harmful effects of white supremacy was how it

destroyed the authority of Black fathers, and Nicholas Buccola told me about what James Baldwin learned by observing
David Baldwin:

> David's life was marked by economic, social, and political
> domination. In the face of this domination, David came
> to hate himself and that self-hatred led him to despise
> the human beings around him. As Baldwin watched his
> father consumed by despair, he made it his mission to
> avoid that fate. The primary means through which Bald-
> win was able to pull off that escape was language. Words
> helped Baldwin make sense of what destroyed his father
> and words helped him figure out what liberation might
> look like.[2]

James Baldwin knew from an early age that he was Black
and that he was smart, and that if he was going to escape the
crippling poverty he and his family endured, the "intolerable
bitterness of spirit" that had killed his father and could also
destroy him, it was going to have to be through that intelligence.[3] As a ten-year-old at P.S. 24 in Harlem, he was mentored
by a young white schoolteacher, Orilla "Bill" Miller, who recognized his writing talent. "She gave me books to read and
talked to me about the books, and about the world," Baldwin remembered.[4] She took him to plays like Orson Welles's
groundbreaking *Black Macbeth* and to movies, all of which
expanded his world, but he also remembered the diminishing
effect their four- or five-year relationship had on his stepfather,
who remained skeptical of Miller despite Emma's characterization of the teacher as truly "Christian." One day, David warned
James, he would realize that a white person could never be his
friend, that white people only wanted to keep Black people

down. But Bill Miller was more than just James's guide to a wider and more artful world; in her generosity and care for him and for his family, he discovered something as formative as his father's despair. "It is certainly because of Bill Miller," he wrote, "that I never really managed to hate white people."[5]

In middle school, Baldwin encountered one of the first of the great Black writers who would shape his future, the poet Countee Cullen, a major figure of the Harlem Renaissance, that flowering of African American artists and writers that took place from 1918 into the 1930s. Baldwin attended DeWitt Clinton High School, a mostly Jewish high school in the Bronx, where he edited the school's magazine with Richard Avedon (later one of America's most famous photographers), and to which he contributed stories, poems, and plays. In high school, Baldwin was introduced to the African American painter Beauford Delaney, who demonstrated how a Black man could be a top-flight artist, and who became a longtime friend and mentor.

Another formative factor of his teenage years was James's powerful encounter with faith. Despite his many difficulties with David Baldwin, James followed his father into ministry, developing into an acclaimed young preacher. Although he did not write out his sermons, the three years he spent in the pulpit clearly helped to make him a writer. But he gradually came to doubt some of the central tenets of the faith he preached, including the exclusive salvation offered only to those who professed Jesus as their savior.

Baldwin remembered how his best friend from high school had come over for a visit, and that afterward David Baldwin had asked him if his friend was a Christian. When James told him no, that he was Jewish, David slapped him across the face, and James, furious, wondered if he was supposed to be "glad that a friend of mine, or anyone, was to be tormented forever in Hell."

"He's a better Christian than you are," Baldwin told his father and walked out of the house, the battle between them now, at last, out in the open.[6]

Later, this Jewish friend Emile helped Baldwin to leave the church by challenging him to sneak out of services and attend a Broadway matinee with him. Baldwin remembered that friendship between adolescent boys as extraordinary, for Emile confronted him in this way: "Even if what I was preaching was gospel, I had no right to preach it if I no longer believed it." To stay in the church because he was afraid of it was cowardice, "unutterably far beneath me." At 1:15 on the appointed Sunday, Baldwin snuck out of the service to meet Emile, and "that was how I left the church."[7]

At age eighteen, after high school, James set aside his plans for further education to help his family survive and to live on his own. He took various jobs, including work for the New Jersey railroad. On the same day in 1943, David Baldwin died and James's eighth sibling was born. James moved to Greenwich Village, where he worked, wrote, fell in love with both men and women, and engaged the attention of the African American novelist Richard Wright, who helped him secure a major grant that allowed him to focus on his writing. Baldwin began publishing his work in national magazines like *The Nation, Partisan Review*, and *Commentary*, but America continued to feel like a place where Baldwin could not live freely as a Black man or as a gay man. The suicide of a beloved friend haunted him, and he cycled between grief and rage. He worried, as Nicholas Buccola explains, that if he stayed in the United States he would follow his friend and his father down the path to self-destruction.[8] And so in 1948, with forty dollars in his pocket, Baldwin boarded a boat to France and launched himself down another path, that of an American expatriate living and working in Paris.

Paris after World War II welcomed African American artists, singers, and writers, as indeed it always had. The dancer and actress Josephine Baker had taken the town by storm in the 1920s, and Baldwin's benefactor Richard Wright had, in turn, been treated as an honored guest in Paris, a significant man of letters. Wright wrote his American editor that there was so little racial hatred in France "that it seems a little unreal."[9] Baldwin—the James Baldwin we would now know and recognize—became himself in St-Germain on the Left Bank of the Seine. Freed from the church and from his family's watching eyes, he made friends, debated literature and thought, lived into his sexuality, and slowly began to make a name for himself as a writer and to make progress on his first novel.

A part of Baldwin's claiming his own identity was coming to grips with the groundbreaking work of Richard Wright, the first truly important Black American novelist. In what felt, I'm sure, like betrayal to Wright, Baldwin's first major essay, "Everybody's Protest Novel," compared Wright's *Native Son* to ungainly propaganda novels like *Uncle Tom's Cabin*. However well-intentioned the protest novel might be, Baldwin wrote, the truest job of the novelist is to represent human life in all its beauty, complication, and difficulty, not simply to convey a message. In rejecting Wright as his artistic father, he was also claiming his own path, and relationships between fathers and sons were on his mind as he continued to labor at his novel, as, indeed, they would continue to be for the rest of his life.

Paris was not all glistening lights and acclaim. Baldwin was virtually penniless and struggled with depression. But in Paris, he met perhaps the great love of his life, a young Swiss artist named Lucien Happersberger. Lucien's family had a chalet in the Swiss village of Leukerbad/Loèche-les-Bains, and he took Baldwin there in late 1951 and early 1952. Two seminal events happened that first winter in Leukerbad: there in the Swiss Alps, Baldwin finished the novel he now called *Go Tell It on the Mountain* (1953), which would make his name, and he also received an epiphany about race and prejudice in this village where he was the first person of color the villagers had ever seen. In his essay "Stranger in the Village" (which appears in the 1955 collection, *Notes of a Native Son*), Baldwin argued that white Americans did not have the luxury of treating American Black people as exotic; their destinies were tied together. African Americans could not simply go back down the mountain and disappear. It was a revelation that led to his lifelong insistence that racism in America was a problem the races would have to solve together, for their own good, and that love, not hatred and violence, represented the only possible solution for those who were condemned or destined to live together.

Baldwin's second novel, *Giovanni's Room* (1956), was considered daring for its homoerotic content, although Baldwin himself said that the point of the book was not that its narrator David loves a man, but that he doesn't love him enough. David narrates the entire novel on what he describes as the darkest night of his life, the night before his lover, Giovanni, is to be executed, and the story revolves around his failure to realize the depths of what he had with Giovanni and his own attempts to distance himself from any meaningful relationship.

"*Go Tell It* is not about the Church," Baldwin said in a late interview, "and *Giovanni* isn't really about homosexuality. It's about what happens to you if you're afraid to love anybody."[10] *Giovanni's Room* is now considered an LGBTQ classic, which gave gay readers a voice and an experience to claim as their own. In later novels, Baldwin would continue to explore sexual identity alongside other human identities, writing about diverse casts with sympathy and understanding. By now, Baldwin had also evolved a personal writing style with which to write about these big topics, a combination of African American preaching, the rhythms of the King James Bible, and the stately cadences and laser focus of the American/British writer Henry James, whom Baldwin greatly admired. It was a graceful and powerful voice capable of thoughtful and beautiful reflection.

As the civil rights movement continued, Baldwin reengaged with American life, as he would off and on until his death. He served as a witness to violence and prejudice, becoming one of the movement's most eloquent spokespeople. He wrote major magazine pieces; received thousands of invitations to speak at colleges, churches, and civic groups; and in 1963 published one of the most important books on race ever written in America, *The Fire Next Time*, which spent forty-one weeks on the bestseller lists. During his time in America, Baldwin engaged with Medgar Evers, Martin Luther King Jr., Malcolm X, and many other figures involved in the struggle for rights and full citizenship. In 1963 he convened a group of Black artists, entertainers, and activists to meet with Robert F. Kennedy, then the attorney general for his brother John, and although Robert Kennedy was taken aback by the anger of some of those present and stunned by what he initially perceived as their disloyalty to America, that shock later led him to radical reunderstanding: many of those present felt no loyalty to America because America had manifested no loyalty to them and those who looked like them.

The 1960s represent the high point of James Baldwin's career. He was the topic of conversation at every New York cocktail party; his fiction and essays (especially the best-selling novel *Another Country* [1962] and *The Fire Next Time*) were required reading; he appeared on the cover of *TIME* magazine; and in February 1965 he devastated conservative intellectual

William F. Buckley in a debate at Cambridge University about race and the American Dream.

Although Baldwin continued to write, the assassinations of Malcolm X, King, and Evers (and the Kennedys) leached away his hope for racial change in America, and at the same time he was criticized by some in the Black Power movement for his unwillingness to countenance violence as a tool against oppression. He addressed his disillusionment and attempts to regain his hope in *No Name in the Street* (1972), arguing again that "the truth which frees black people will also free white people, but this is a truth which white people find very difficult to swallow."[11]

Baldwin spent much of the rest of his life at his home in Saint-Paul-de-Vence in southern France, although he never gave up his American citizenship. His works of the 1970s and 1980s did not achieve the same popular notice and critical acclaim as his works of the 1950s and 1960s, and for some, his stature seemed diminished. But he remained an elder statesman of Black culture, a mentor and a friend to artists, scholars, and critics including Maya Angelou, Toni Morrison, Henry Louis Gates, and Amiri Baraka. He also continued to write. In 1979 he proposed to his agent Jay Acton an ambitious (perhaps too ambitious) book on Evers, King, and Malcolm X (it was ultimately imagined as the 2016 documentary film, *I Am Not Your Negro*). His article for *Playboy* on the Atlanta child murders— later published as *The Evidence of Things Not Seen* (1985)—was a searing indictment of continuing racial injustice that dealt with his lifelong issues with his characteristic skill. At the time of his death in 1987 he was working on a play, *The Welcome Table*, that brought together many of his greatest themes. I have seen it and read it; it would have been a fitting end to a monumental life.

James Baldwin's body was laid to rest in the Ferncliff Cemetery in Ardsley, New York, but his work and words remain vibrant and vital. Susan McWilliams wrote in her introduction to *A Political Companion to James Baldwin* that we proceed from Baldwinian Moment to Baldwinian Moment.[12] The election of Barack Obama, the nation's first Black president. The Black Lives Matter movement. Ta-Nehisi Coates's National Book Award–winning memoir *Between the World and Me* (2015), consciously modeled on *The Fire Next Time*. Barry Jenkins's painful and beautiful film adaptation of *If Beale Street Could Talk* (2018). A past president who weaponized racism and anti-immigrant sentiment as a political tool. A virus that quarantined people by nation and neighborhood, and initially struck people of color most violently. The murder of George Floyd. The deaths of other Black men at the hands of white men. And of course, there will be some other Baldwinian moment tomorrow, and the day after, and the day after that. In each of those moments, we turn to Baldwin to help us understand something about the world we inhabit, and something about ourselves.

James Baldwin is as alive in this moment as he has ever been, his voice as clear and measured. And what does he have to teach us?

It is nothing less than a commitment to being fully alive, a way to be fully human, an awareness that love, freedom, and justice are the universal desires of every single human being.

It is a commitment to look at our world and at our lives and to strive to tell nothing but the truth.

Baldwin as Prophet of Humanity

Jill Lepore introduced her acclaimed 2018 history of America, *These Truths*, by introducing us to James Baldwin, which is only appropriate. It is Baldwin, after all, who said, "History is not the past. It is the present. We carry our history with us. We *are* our history," and it is Baldwin who constantly suggests to us how we can use our history instead of being used by it.[1] When we are used by it, when we fail to confront it, to name the sins of the past, to dream of a better future, we are trapped by that history, "cruelly trapped between what we would like to be and what we actually are. And we cannot possibly become what we would like to be until we are willing to ask ourselves just why the lives we lead on this continent are mainly so empty, so tame, and so ugly."[2] But who can have the vision and the courage to see what is, to some eyes, invisible, and to many others, so horrible? It takes a person with insight and wisdom, a person willing to interrogate his own life and the world around him, to tell hard truths and name painful realities.

It takes an artist. A saint.

A prophet.

Gwendolyn Brooks, at the end of her appointment as the US poet laureate in 1986, introduced James Baldwin at the

19

Library of Congress in this fashion: "Many have been called prophets, but here is a bona fide prophet. Long ago, he guaranteed 'the fire next time.' . . . Virtually the following day, we, smelling smoke, looked up and found ourselves surrounded by leering, singeing fire. . . . And no, James Baldwin did not start the fire—he foretold its coming."[3]

For his part, Baldwin had long seen himself in this prophetic role. In 1965 he repeated in the *New York Times* words he had recently said at his Cambridge Union debate with William F. Buckley: that he found himself, "not for the first time, in the position of a kind of Jeremiah." [4]

To people who are not Jewish or Christian—and even to some who are—this statement might be incomprehensible. A kind of Jeremiah? Who—or what—does that mean?

Jeremiah was an Old Testament prophet, a Hebrew visionary who looked at his nation of Judah and saw it riddled with contradictions and hypocrisy. To be a saint in the mode of Jeremiah is to be a witness (which is what the word "martyr" literally means in New Testament Greek): to see the world and to tell the truth, regardless of its personal cost. In his Temple Sermon, Jeremiah condemned his nation, which saw itself as a chosen people, and he told them that unless they evinced a love for justice, God would never abide among them:

> The word that came to Jeremiah from the Lord: Stand in the gate of the Lord's house, and proclaim there this word, and say, Hear the word of the Lord, all you people of Judah, you that enter these gates to worship the Lord. Thus says the Lord of hosts, the God of Israel: Amend your ways and your doings, and let me dwell with you in this place. Do not trust in these deceptive words: "This

is the temple of the Lord, the temple of the Lord, the
temple of the Lord."

For if you truly amend your ways and your doings, if you
truly act justly one with another, if you do not oppress the
alien, the orphan, and the widow, or shed innocent blood
in this place, and if you do not go after other gods to your
own hurt, then I will dwell with you in this place, in the
land that I gave of old to your ancestors forever and ever.[5]

In this sermon, Jeremiah tasked a religious nation for the
many ways it failed to live up to its calling, and Baldwin understood that to be his own task when he claimed the mantle of a
Jeremiah. Baldwin had been a renowned popular preacher in
Harlem in his teen years, and although he turned away from
the formal faith of his youth, he still spoke and wrote and
understood experience through the Judeo-Christian metaphors,
stories, and rhetoric he had absorbed growing up in the church.

But truth be told, you do not need to be Jewish or Christian
to understand the twin poles of regret and hope at work in this
distinctive discourse, which is not limited simply to religious
failings. For some four hundred years, American Jeremiahs have
shaped our national identity and direction by speaking out
about whatever they have seen going wrong in the American
experiment. Initially these jeremiads were preached by Puritan
divines like Samuel Danforth and Increase and Cotton Mather,
but many pastors, activists, and writers since have delivered both
sacred and secular jeremiads about how, if we do not change our
ways, America is destined for ruin.

Sacvan Bercovitch, a literary and cultural critic who studied
the roots of American exceptionalism, argued in his influential
1978 monograph *The American Jeremiad* that American prophets

have long taken the nation to task for falling short of its ideals, for its sins of commission and omission—but also have held out the hope of some sort of salvation if, as Jeremiah preached, we truly amend our ways and our doings, if we truly act justly one with another. From Jonathan Edwards to F. Scott Fitzgerald, from Langston Hughes to Toni Morrison, this most prominent form of American rhetoric has centered on those dual explorations of failure and promise. Wen Stephenson noted in the *New York Times* that "we Americans, the jeremiad proclaims, have failed to live up to our founding principles, betrayed our sacred covenant as history's (or God's) chosen nation, and must rededicate ourselves to our ideals, reclaim our founding promise."[6] It is late. But perhaps, as Baldwin suggests, it's not too late to become the people or the nation we are called to be.

To be a Jeremiah means to call your people to account, something Baldwin constantly but lovingly did on questions of race and justice and identity and culture. He wrote in *Notes of a Native Son* that "I love America more than any other country in this world, and, exactly for this reason, I insist on the right to criticize her perpetually."[7] That perpetual criticism may have been necessary; Baldwin observed that white Americans, desperate to maintain their delusions and their innocence, "find it difficult, if not impossible, to learn anything worth learning."[8] There is a reason prophets have to keep calling at the top of their lungs; if people were ready to listen and change, one warning would be sufficient.

Baldwin testified that America continued to fall short, but to the end of his days he did not completely rule out the possibility of future success. In fact, the history of American prophets, from the Matherses to Henry David Thoreau, from John Steinbeck to Martin Luther King Jr. to the present, suggests that this critical attention to our deepest values and willingness to

face our shared history offer the greatest possibility for transformation. Yes, we have fallen short, and if we continue on our
present path, we court destruction. But if we turn from our
wicked ways, if we embrace the possibility of change, we may
still become something greater, kinder, more beautiful than we
are—may, in fact, become something that some people would
call worthy of being "American."

Or more important, still: of being called human.

I have had some of the words from William Faulkner's
Nobel Prize acceptance speech on my office door at Baylor University for over thirty years because they speak to the job that
people like me take on. Here is what Mr. Faulkner said on that
occasion (speaking mostly in the masculine pronoun, since that
is what people did in 1950):

> Our tragedy today is a general and universal physical fear
> so long sustained by now that we can even bear it. There
> are no longer problems of the spirit. There is only the
> question: When will I be blown up? Because of this, the
> young man or woman writing today has forgotten the
> problems of the human heart in conflict with itself which
> alone can make good writing because only that is worth
> writing about, worth the agony and the sweat.
>
> He must learn them again. He must teach himself
> that the basest of all things is to be afraid; and, teach-
> ing himself that, forget it forever, leaving no room in his
> workshop for anything but the old verities and truths
> of the heart, the old universal truths lacking which any
> story is ephemeral and doomed—love and honor and
> pity and pride and compassion and sacrifice. . . .
>
> I decline to accept the end of man. It is easy enough to
> say that man is immortal simply because he will endure:

that when the last dingdong of doom has clanged and faded from the last worthless rock hanging tideless in the last red and dying evening, that even then there will still be one more sound: that of his puny inexhaustible voice, still talking.

I refuse to accept this. I believe that man will not merely endure: he will prevail. He is immortal, not because he alone among creatures has an inexhaustible voice, but because he has a soul, a spirit capable of compassion and sacrifice and endurance. The poet's, the writer's, duty is to write about these things. It is his privilege to help man endure by lifting his heart, by reminding him of the courage and honor and hope and pride and compassion and pity and sacrifice which have been the glory of his past. The poet's voice need not merely be the record of man, it can be one of the props, the pillars to help him endure and prevail.[9]

I like this speech more than Baldwin did, because Faulkner got something right: "the old universal truths lacking which any story is ephemeral and doomed—love and honor and pity and pride and compassion and sacrifice." Great artists, poets, and writers are not great simply because they're distinctive— although they are distinctive—but because they also offer the species something universal. They teach us something about our own humanity out of the distinctive humanity that they inhabit. In other words, one does not have to be gay or Black or urban or expatriate or a faithful struggler to learn what James Baldwin has to teach us, and as we will see, he knew it.

Sharifa Rhodes-Pitt has described a rhetorical turn that Baldwin constantly performed in his writing. She calls it "The Jimmy."[10] In "The Jimmy," Baldwin shifts from his own postage stamp of land to the great universal truths and, in the process, proves how a great artist can be a unique individual, but can also help all of us understand important truths about our own unique selves.

We are all better than our worst acts.

We are always in a state of becoming.

We are each looking for the place we belong and the people who will love and understand us.

And we need the help of writers, artists, priests, and prophets to find those things.

A few closing notes. First, while like Baldwin I'll often be writing here about prejudice directed against Black people by white people, or at gay people by straight people, I hope all of us can acknowledge that anyone who is a straight white Christian male in this culture has benefited from a set of prejudices that have built hierarchies to exclude or diminish others. The principle of intersectionality means that you may have experienced elements of the prejudices Baldwin and I talk about because of your identity as a woman, or as a trans woman, or as an Indigenous woman. All oppressed people deserve to have their experiences recognized, but I focus primarily on white-on-Black racism because of America's dismal history of chattel slavery, repression, and racial violence experienced by Black people—and because this was such an important part of Baldwin's lived experience.

Second, as often as I can, I'm going to offer up James Baldwin's actual words and arguments. While necessarily this book demonstrates me reading Baldwin, I'm not interested in simply presenting a Jimmy Baldwin who agrees with me on every topic. That would defeat the purpose of a wisdom book on his work, and it would ignore the ways he has shaped and changed me across the years. I've tried to listen to Baldwin's words, to let him teach me what he had to say, not to try to fit them into some framework of my own devising. Even though the shock of recognizing yourself in a writer's work can feel like a splash of icy water—or a slap—I'm most interested in the Baldwin who challenges, teaches, and encourages me to do better. To *be* better.

I hope you are too.

So what gods will we serve, what stories will inform us, what prophets will shape us? Let us step forward together and discover what Blessed St. James of Harlem, patron saint of the journey, has to offer us.

Baldwin on Culture

Then they all gathered around Sonny and Sonny
played.... Sonny's fingers filled the air
with life, his life. But that life contained so many
others.... I understood at last that he
could help us to be free if we would listen, that
we would never be free until we did.

—James Baldwin, "Sonny's Blues"

For years now, I have been requiring my film classes at Baylor University to begin by reading *The Devil Finds Work*, James Baldwin's 1976 book-length essay on race and culture. Before we watch a frame of film, before we've introduced a single cinematic term, my students read, mark, and inwardly digest Baldwin's thoughts about how movies work, what they represent, what we can learn from them for good and ill, and how Baldwin—operating out of his singular identity as well as his artistic sensibility—responded to specific films. It's a masterpiece of criticism, as well as a plain old artistic masterpiece,

shaped to a sharp point as he concludes with—and dismisses—
the hit film *The Exorcist* (1973) as pure American escapism:
"The mindless and hysterical banality of the evil presented in
The Exorcist is the most terrifying thing about the film. The
Americans should certainly know more about evil than that; if
they pretend otherwise, they are lying, and any black man, and
not only blacks ... can call them on this lie; he who has been
treated as the devil recognizes the devil when they meet."[1] It's
a powerful conclusion to a book filled with thoughtful evalua-
tions and attempts to understand American culture through its
art, to understand how art speaks and misspeaks to us.

The Devil Finds Work is criticism as gift and challenge, criticism in service of truth and in service of justice, and it is James
Baldwin as the world first encountered him, the thoughtful,
fierce, and idealistic observer of culture who demanded that art
show us ourselves as we are, all of us in our full humanity. In
an essay on his friend the painter Beauford Delaney, Baldwin
talked about how Delaney's art, through the reality of Delaney's
seeing, "caused me to begin to see."[2] After we read and discuss
The Devil Finds Work, I always find my students asking, "What
Baldwin books should I read next?" His vision has expanded
theirs, and they want to see more still.

For Baldwin, art, literature, and culture are central ways
we understand ourselves and the world we occupy, and so he
held his roles as artist and critic to be sacred. From his earliest
book reviews, in essays like the widely read "Everyone's Protest
Novel," published in the *Partisan Review* in 1949 when he was
just twenty-four years old, and in his feuds with elder authors
like Richard Wright, Baldwin was demanding novels, plays, and
films that in some way represented him—and all of us—without sentimentalizing or brutalizing, works of art that could call

for social change without being only about their issues. Baldwin was a courageous critic, demanding more and better, as in the aforementioned *The Devil Finds Work*, which critic Noah Berlatsky lovingly describes as Baldwin's attempt "to reconcile the cinema he loves, which represents the country he loves, with its duplicity and faithlessness."[3]

Most importantly, much like his contemporary the Catholic novelist and essayist Walker Percy, who held strong beliefs about the "diagnostic novel" and its personal and social functions, Baldwin believed that great art should take on the sicknesses and psychoses of those who consume it, show them their flaws and failings, and offer them the chance to become well, to help those readers, listeners, and viewers to live into their full humanity.[4] Baldwin said that a great artist was in a loving war with his culture, "and he does, at his best, what lovers do, which is to reveal the beloved to himself, and with that revelation, make freedom real."[5] The great challenge for all of us, Baldwin wrote in *Giovanni's Room* (1956), "is to say Yes to life"—just as, at the conclusion of *The Devil Finds Work*, he suggests that we see the devil in that moment "when no other human being is real for you, nor are you real for yourself."[6] Revelation engenders reality.

As a critic, as in his own novels and plays, Baldwin's project was to make readers real to themselves, to say Yes to life, and as Nicholas Buccola puts it, to force them to thoughtfully "examine the racial, religious, and sexual mythologies" that dominate their lives.[7] Great art can help us become something other than we are, but first it has to honestly show us ourselves in a way that we can accept and from which we can learn. Baldwin is a guide for us in that process. Here we explore three major questions about art and culture that he took on as writer and critic, and approach some practical considerations.

- What can art (good and bad) teach us about what makes good art? (And what, exactly, makes art more or less successful?)
- What can great art teach us about our culture? (And what does it mean for an artist to be a witness to that culture?)
- What can great art teach us about ourselves? (And how does art help us to be fully human?)

Although over the years Baldwin took plenty of writing to task for what he perceived as its failings, he defined the job of the artist in positive ways as well. In the original "Autobiographical Notes" to *Notes of a Native Son* (1955), he argued that "this is the only real concern of the artist, to recreate out of the disorder of life the order which is art."[8] In "The Creative Process," he wrote that the artist's function is to plumb "the mystery of the human being."[9] In an essay on the works of William Shakespeare, "This Nettle, Danger . . . ," he said the task is to "operate as an unimpeachable witness to one's own experience."[10] In a 1964 essay, "Words of a Native Son," written for *Playboy* at the height of his acclaim, he put it this way: "Every artist is involved with one single effort, really, which is to dig down to where reality is."[11] In these and a number of equally arresting formulations of the task of the artist, Baldwin is saying different things that end up landing in the same quadrant: art is about life, love, and telling the truth, and art that doesn't do that divides us from each other and from ourselves instead of uniting us.

Over the course of his forty-year writing career, beginning with essays and reviews in the early 1940s and concluding with essential writings gathered in the posthumous film and book *I Am Not Your Negro* (2016/2017), Baldwin was challenging artists and consumers of art to represent human experience in all the beautiful complexity he knew and ultimately demanded of his own work. Before he had created his own important creative fiction and dramatic writing, his critical essays for publications like *New Leader*, *The Nation*, and *Commentary* were showing how he might proceed and inspiring him to do the same.

That trust from magazine editors was an important part of his development. As Baldwin biographer Douglas Field notes, "For a young African American with no formal education after the age of seventeen, these editors, Baldwin suggests, saved or at least ignited his life as a writer."[12] That patronage from liberal editors who commissioned reviews and essays was important, but it was also limiting, and would ultimately shape Baldwin's approach to his own writing and that of others. Critic Hilton Als, writing an appreciation of Baldwin for the *New Yorker*, suggests that "these editors supported Baldwin's growth as a critic and allowed him access to the social world of New York intellectuals, but their patronage was not without its restrictions: as a black, he was expected and encouraged to review black books."[13]

This limitation seemed patronizing to Baldwin himself, even as he acknowledged the great gift he had been given as an unlettered young person. "That was a very nice atmosphere for me; in a sense it saved me from despair. But most of the books I reviewed were Be Kind to Niggers, Be Kind to Jews, while America was going through one of its liberal convulsions.... Thousands of such tracts were published during those years and it seems to me I had to read every single one of them; the color of my skin made me an expert," he explained, adding,

> And so, when I got to Paris, I had to discharge all that, which was really the reason for my essay, "Everybody's Protest Novel." I was convinced then—and I still am— that those sorts of books do nothing but bolster up an image. All of this had quite a bit to do with the direction I

took as a writer, because it seemed to me that if I took the role of a victim then I was simply reassuring the defenders of the status quo; as long as I was a victim they could pity me and add a few more pennies to my home-relief check.[14]

Early on, this ghettoed artistic experience led Baldwin to define his approach to art—and what art should and should not be doing—at least by negation. This is a natural step on the way to defining how art should work. I began writing professionally about music and movies in my late teens and twenties, and I can tell you that a young reviewer often feels more comfortable saying, *I don't know for sure what great art is, but I know that this ain't it.* When we define by negation, we set up some parameters that allow us to think toward a positive opposing pole, or a multitude of better options, all of them avoiding the perils of what Baldwin saw as a limited or inartistic depiction of the human experience.

Artists of any kind have often compared themselves with those who came before, defining themselves in opposition to those artists, and claiming a new space of originality and creativity for themselves and those they see as fellow travelers. So it is that the nineteenth-century American realist writer Mark Twain savages James Fenimore Cooper for what he sees as the ridiculous excesses of Romantic literature in works like Cooper's *The Deerslayer*:

A work of art? It has no invention; it has no order, system, sequence, or result; it has no lifelikeness, no thrill, no stir, no seeming of reality; its characters are confusedly drawn, and by their acts and words they prove that they are not the sort of people the author claims that they are;

its humor is pathetic; its pathos is funny; its conversations are—oh! indescribable; its love-scenes odious; its
English a crime against the language.[15]

Twain was patently unfair to judge Cooper's novels by his
own literary standards, just as it would be unfair for artists and
writers of the Renaissance to judge works of the Middle Ages
as deficient based on new understandings of perspective and
humanism, just as it would be unfair for Impressionists like
Mary Cassatt or Claude Monet to hector classical Salon paint-
ers like François Joseph Heim for not capturing the momentary
shifts in light and shadow that defined their Impressionist art.
Such attempts to define what art should be are personal, and
typically are about a revision or rejection of previous efforts in
favor of what a writer, artist, or filmmaker is attempting in the
moment. This is only natural; each generation reacts against the
one before it.

Sydney Krause, in his book *Mark Twain as Critic*, argues
that "Twain's pointing with alarm to Cooper's literary offenses
was more than a caveat against the pitfalls of romantic fiction; it was a plea for readers to accept the verdict of history
that old-style romanticism—at best an exotic movement with
a code of feeling engendered by a cult of sensibility, to which
America opposed the cult of experience—that this brand of die-
hard romanticism was a literary dead letter in post–Civil War
America."[16] This attack by Twain on his eminent predecessor
was nothing more nor less than a defense of the writing Twain
had done and was doing as superior to any American writing
that had been popular before Twain arrived on the scene. By
attacking Cooper's Romantic art, Twain was able to delineate
his own aesthetic success and claim his own preeminence. (Not
surprisingly, later writers and activists criticized Baldwin for

what they saw as his failures, again claiming space for themselves at the expense of their ancestor. It's what we do.)

None of this is necessarily fair, and in some cases, it can appear to be a betrayal, as many believe of Baldwin's criticism of novelist Richard Wright, who had blazed a trail for Black writers and who had served as a personal mentor for Baldwin. Hilton Als—who writes about how he himself has wrestled to carve out artistic space separate from Baldwin—describes how in the important early essay "Everybody's Protest Novel" attacking Wright's *Native Son*, "Baldwin meant not only to bury the tradition of black letters which had its roots in a Communism supported by white dilettantes but also to supersede Wright as the one black writer worth reading in the largely white world of American letters."[17] The Baldwin essay is classic artist behavior, Oedipus overthrowing his father, but as Als admits, Baldwin also expresses genuine critical objections to the elder writer's work. In saying what he did not think fiction should do—perhaps especially by pointing out examples in his mentor's popular and widely acclaimed novel—Baldwin expresses his own aesthetic of what art should be and do, even if he begins by negation.

Baldwin opens "Everybody's Protest Novel" by inveighing against Harriet Beecher Stowe's *Uncle Tom's Cabin* (1852), a novel he'd read and reread (along with Charles Dickens's *A Tale of Two Cities*) as a child. It is, he says rightly, "a very bad novel, having, in its self-righteous, virtuous sentimentality, much in common with *Little Women*." He then goes on to define and discuss sentimentality, which for him is a cardinal literary sin since it relies on stock situations and dishonest emotional appeals to command the reader's attention. "The wet eyes of the sentimentalist," he concludes, "betray his aversion to experience, his fear of life, his arid heart; and it is always therefore, the signal of secret and violent inhumanity, the mask of cruelty."[18]

A writer who appeals to the reader by appealing to a shared experience rather than by creating an expertly written scene is lazy, we might say, but Baldwin went further, arguing that it represented an avoidance of real life on the part of both story-teller and audience. I agree: over my three decades of teaching fiction and screenwriting I have often had to advise students that some situations are so fraught with inherent emotion (the death of a child or perhaps a beloved pet) that to use them inartistically is to commit a crime against both literature and humanity. The exaggerated violence in *Uncle Tom's Cabin*, Baldwin argued, was an example of sentimentality, since all of us can agree that extreme cruelty to another is bad. Where is the art or epiphany in that?

Then he goes further. By treating Uncle Tom, for example, simply as an exemplar of Christian charity, rather than depicting him as a fully rounded character, Ms. Stowe succeeds in her aim of proving that slavery is odious, but by rounding off the humanity of the character, in some ways she demonstrates the precise opposite. "In overlooking, denying, evading his complexity—which is nothing more than the disquieting complexity of ourselves—we are diminished and we perish; only within this web of ambiguity, paradox, this hunger, danger, darkness, can we find ourselves and the power that will free us from ourselves."[19]

In his rejection of easy lessons, of stereotypes, and of sentimentalism, Baldwin is staking out a claim for realism, honesty, and complexity as literary values. *Uncle Tom's Cabin* would be—and was—an effective pamphlet for the antislavery cause, he argues, but it is an execrable novel.

The linking of Wright's *Native Son* with *Uncle Tom's Cabin* upset many writers of both Wright's and Baldwin's generations. Eldridge Cleaver responded by saying that Baldwin criticized

Wright and Bigger Thomas because Baldwin possessed "the most grueling, agonizing, total hatred of the black, particularly himself, and the most shameful, sycophantic love of the whites."[20] Wright, furious about the publication of "Everybody's Protest Novel," is supposed to have told Baldwin that all literature is protest (perhaps, Baldwin said he responded, but not all protest is literature).[21] But Baldwin saw the resemblance between the two books as—to him—a fatal weakness of both.

Harriet Beecher Stowe's Uncle Tom and Richard Wright's Bigger Thomas could not be more different in their outlooks and actions, but these protagonists were depicted similarly and for similar reasons. As Kichung Kim writes, "Because of his color and background Bigger Thomas is robbed of his humanity, and is made into a mere bearer of the black man's fear, hatred and anger directed against the white society."[22] Both men, Tom and Thomas, are stereotypes and retellings of white myths about Black men, even if they are distinctly opposite racist myths (the Good Black Man and the Black Beast). Myths are useful organizing tools, but they are never human. We are all gloriously complicated beings, carrying good and bad, breaking out of molds, surprising ourselves and others.

As a writer, teacher, and preacher, I am drawn to Walt Whitman's lines from *Song of Myself* because they encompass my understanding of our complex humanity:

> *Do I contradict myself?*
> *Very well then I contradict myself,*
> *(I am large, I contain multitudes.)*[23]

Only this contradiction, this complication can accurately represent human existence.

Like Whitman, Baldwin excoriates art that sentimentalizes, simplifies, or stereotypes, even when it does so for noble reasons. The protest novel has, Baldwin admits, an important purpose: "to bring greater freedom to the oppressed." As we have seen and will see, this was a central goal of Baldwin himself in his life and in his activism. But in literature, he suggests that nobility of purpose is no excuse for infelicity of style and infidelity to life. Works such as *Uncle Tom's Cabin* and *Native Son* are, he argues, confined to the social realm, where they are divorced from the true power of great literature, simply "fantasies, connecting nowhere with reality, sentimental."[24]

Baldwin has similar thoughts about the groundbreaking 1967 movie *Guess Who's Coming to Dinner* and its characters, including Dr. John Wade Prentice, the character portrayed by Sidney Poitier. Dr. Prentice is a world-renowned physician who has fallen in love with a white woman and gone home to San Francisco with her to meet her parents. This perfect character ("the word 'prodigy' is simply ridiculously inadequate," Baldwin says, and he later dubs Prentice "the wonder doctor") is not so much a character as a function, a myth created to make white audiences able to accept the interracial romance that drives the story.[25] Stereotyped, too, is the character of Tillie, played by Isabel Sanford. She is the Black maid who has helped raise the daughter, is referred to as "one of the family"—a familiar and comforting myth about slaves and servants—and regards herself as the protector of the daughter against this uppity Negro who doesn't know his place. Black theologian Kelly Brown Douglas, with whom I have screened and discussed this film in Washington National Cathedral and around the globe, asks of this scene something I have often used as a rubric for approaching every narrative about race and prejudice: "Why do you suppose a white audience needed this?"

Baldwin is very clear about why he believes white audiences in 1967 needed a Black character like Tillie, a stock character he calls a "faithful retainer": because she could take radical notions and attack them from her raced identity, thus letting white people off the hook in the same way that Stowe's depiction of Uncle Tom lets white people ease back into their familiar lives: "How many times have we seen her! She is Dilsey, she is Mammy, in *Gone with the Wind*, and in *Imitation of Life*, and *The Member of the Wedding*—mother of sorrows, whore and saint.... The film seems to be using her to suggest that backward people can be found on both sides of the racial fence—a point which can scarcely be made so long as one is sitting on it."[26] A stereotype and a simplification, her presence in the film is also a mythic lie, for this "member of the family" spends the entire film preparing the titular dinner, and when at last supper is finally announced, please be assured that there is no seat prepared for her at the table. She will be serving, as she always does, this white family to whom she is unreasonably devoted. Tillie's character constitutes a powerful racial statement that the liberal white director and screenwriter of *Guess Who's Coming to Dinner* unintentionally plant in the midst of their film intended to promote equality and equity.

Judging from Baldwin's negative statements about bad art, we might infer that artists shouldn't create a work out of the intention to change the world; they should create a work that accurately reflects the world in which we live.

In teaching fiction writing at Baylor for over thirty years, I have often had students who wanted to convert the world to their point of view—to write pamphlets, as Baldwin would put it—about Jesus, politics, tolerance, or what have you. Some of those points of view I agreed with, as indeed Baldwin agrees that oppression of Black people, of any people, is a horror and must be changed. But as I tell my students, a person who exists in a story only to carry a protest sign is not a character; a character is a human being in whom we can recognize ourselves and our own complex natures, a person who carries brokenness but who nonetheless aspires and hopes to do and be better. As Baldwin put it in a late interview, "I know that we can be better than we are. That's the sum total of my wisdom in all these years."[27]

So it is that we arrive at some understanding of Baldwin's aesthetic, his argument that bad art minimizes and sentimentalizes complex human emotions, and good art creates a complex world populated by complex characters, that good art enlarges us but bad art, even if it espouses opinions that engage us, encages us. Consider Uncle Tom, a simplistic figure who operates almost entirely as a Christ figure in *Uncle Tom's Cabin*. His purpose is to suffer and die to demonstrate the unchristian and inhumane nature of his captivity and his captors. When his good white master George finds Tom dying from the flogging he was given by his sadistic white master Simon Legree, Tom tells him that he is bound for heaven, and when Legree looks in on him, Stowe consciously evokes the words of forgiveness uttered by Jesus on the cross:

> At this moment, Legree sauntered up to the door of the shed, looked in, with a dogged air of affected carelessness, and turned away.
>
> "The old satan!" said George, in his indignation. "It's a comfort to think the devil will pay him for this, some of these days!"
>
> "O, don't!,—oh, ye mustn't!" said Tom, grasping his hand; "he's a poor mis'able critter! It's awful to think on't! O, if he only could repent, the Lord would forgive him now; but I'm 'feared he never will!"

"I hope he won't!" said George; "I never want to see him in heaven!"

"Hush, Mas'r George!—it worries me! Don't feel so! He an't done me no real harm,—only opened the gate of the kingdom for me; that's all!"[28]

Contrast this scene of acceptance and noble suffering with Baldwin's depiction of Fonny and Tish, the lead characters in his 1974 novel, *If Beale Street Could Talk*. The two young lovers live in a society that looks down on them for their Blackness, and Fonny has been unjustly charged with a crime and remains in jail.

One of Baldwin's themes, too, is the unchristian and inhumane nature of Fonny's captivity and his captors, but Fonny and Tish are treated as fully rounded human beings, people with failings and struggles and triumphs, and not simply as literary bumper-stickers to prove a point. Fonny endures his imprisonment, but he doesn't pretend it is a blessing, nor does Tish, who says early in the novel, "I hope that nobody has ever had to look at somebody they love through glass."[29]

And how should people react to a society that treats them as Other and lesser, as subhuman even? Stowe's Tom takes that derision and violence and offers it up as Christian suffering, but Tish feels the injustices and responds in real human indignation. Tish says, for instance, "The people responsible for these jails should be ashamed." And, "I'm not ashamed of Fonny. If anything, I'm proud. He's a man. You can tell by the way he's taken all this shit that he's a man." But Tish remains real: "Sometimes, I admit, I'm scared—because nobody can take the shit they throw on us forever."[30]

I know that enslaved people held these or similar thoughts (I have been teaching Frederick Douglass's autobiography for thirty years), and that oppressed people around the globe hold them, and it is easy to imagine that a person such as Uncle Tom could do so as well. But the character of Uncle Tom in *Uncle Tom's Cabin* does not seem to wrestle with these doubts and fears, to recognize or acknowledge just how difficult life can be, and moreover, we are never given insight into his inner life or suspect that he has one. Even if his entire being revolves around an intense and authentic Christian faith, we are given no glimpse of doubt or suffering. Jesus himself called out to his father from the cross, "Why have you forsaken me?"

Characters who endure intense pain and degradation and never feel their degradation are inhuman; so too is a character like Bigger Thomas who hates, and rapes, and kills, who has no inkling of a better, higher existence.

James Baldwin could say to his nephew that white people "set you down in a ghetto in which, in fact, it intended that you should perish."[31] Ayana Mathis notes of major characters from Black writers like Jean Toomer and Zora Neale Hurston that "Unlike Bigger Thomas, they are robust and nuanced characters—not caricatures endlessly acting out the pathologies of race.... And this is significant, because when black writers affirmed their black subjects' full humanity, the scope of their novels included the expectation that the real world would change radically so that it too could affirm and acknowledge that humanity."[32] To languish without hope, to hate without relief, is to lose one's humanity. Baldwin intended that his nephew James (and, indeed, all people) should have an entire human experience, one not limited like Bigger's to reflexive and bestial responses to violence and degradation.

It is important, Baldwin knew, not to allow the anger and the injustice to overwhelm the art. When Baldwin wrote that Harriet Beecher Stowe "was not so much a novelist as an impassioned pamphleteer," he was saying that the emotion and the outrage Mrs. Stowe felt about slavery was central to what she wrote.[33] But that does not make it successful writing. This is precisely why I often tell my creative writing students, moved by their desires to save souls or save the world, that it's important not to say too much, to shout too loud, to give speeches. Sometimes the art is in what is not being said—or not being said yet.

But then it was so startling for me to read the initial typescript of Baldwin's play *Blues for Mister Charlie* (1964) in the Robert Park Mills papers at the Harry Ransom Humanities Center in my hometown of Austin, Texas. In the draft of the third act of that play, a scene between a Black student, Jimmy; a white newspaper editor, Parnell; and the lead character, Richard, a young militant Black man just back from the North, explodes into anger, recrimination, and yes, speeches. Characters—Richard mostly—say everything that is on their minds. Injustices are held up and loudly decried. Jimmy explains that he is fighting for his civil rights so that he "can raise my children in freedom." It is powerful and painful, and it is also all just too much.[34]

Baldwin and his collaborators must have recognized this. The scene was cut from the play and does not appear in the published version. Baldwin the prophet and rabble-rouser took second place to Baldwin the artist—but in the process, the play's political points, its human insights, shine that much brighter. These changes make it possible for readers and viewers of *Blues for Mister Charlie* to lean into the possibility of their own changes without being overwhelmed by them.

Great art makes transformation possible. It allows us to recognize the full humanity even of characters radically different from ourselves. Tish and Fonny and their families in *Beale Street* do not share my racial or social identity, David and

Giovanni in *Giovanni's Room* do not share my sexual identity, and John, Gabriel, Elizabeth, and Florence in *Go Tell It on the Mountain* do not share my racial, social, or religious identities, yet I see myself reflected in all of them, just as I can see their humanity because of the rich and complex ways in which Baldwin depicts them.

So what would Baldwin say that art teaches about what makes good art?

Good art liberates us rather than enslaving or deluding us. It lets us see humankind in its full complexity, not as some simplified stereotype. It lets us see ourselves as we are and in fact teaches us something about ourselves because it is about life in all its beautiful, painful glory. It tells the truth and serves as a witness, that word that strikes Baldwin as supremely important in a number of realms. At his best, Baldwin's art exemplifies all of these: certainly, the three Baldwin novels I just cited do that good work, as do his plays *Blues for Mister Charlie* and *The Welcome Table*, the screenplay *One Day When I Was Lost*, and the short stories "Sonny's Blues" and "Going to Meet the Man."

With all that said—that Baldwin argues that great art is about human beings and their authentic struggles while inferior art presents a simplified version of reality intended to prove a point—he also never doubted that his writing should teach readers something about their culture and its history. He hoped his work could question some of the dangerous myths presented through art and culture for hundreds of years, even if it did so in a different fashion than the protest novel. One of Baldwin's definitions of artists is that they can serve as an unimpeachable witness to their own experience, which requires that they accept their vision of the world, "no matter how radically this vision departs from that of others."[35] And one of the benefits of

Baldwin's lived experience—Black, gay, artistic, exile—was that it offered him the opportunity to evaluate and reevaluate an America that was primarily white, heterosexual, economically and politically ascendant, and supremely confident.

We spoke at the outset of the long history of the American jeremiad, of artists, writers, singers, and preachers calling on America to account for its sins and failures. But we have not and do not want to be told we are wrong. We don't like being held accountable. And we blame others. *I never enslaved anyone.* Despite Socrates's dictum that the unexamined life is not worth living, the American experience remains largely unexamined, marked by an ignorance, blindness, and intellectual dishonesty against which another great American writer, Henry David Thoreau, railed in *Walden.*

Baldwin observes that "Europeans refer to Americans as children in the same way that American Negroes refer to them as children.... They mean that Americans have so little experience—experience referring not to what happens, but to *who*—that they have no key to the experiences of others."[36] By Americans, Baldwin means white Americans, and by referring to their lack of understanding about the experiences of others, he is highlighting the myths and stories of white supremacy and white superiority that are the largely unexamined underpinnings of much mainstream art.

This situation doesn't hold true for America alone, by the way, but in other parts of the primarily white world as well. Black theologian Anthony Reddie notes a presupposition in British schools and universities about the canon of works to be taught: "It's called 'whiteness.'"[37]

Art that upholds this status quo has a tendency to reinforce people who look like me in our suppositions, just as they have a tendency to denigrate the lived experience of all those who don't look or live like me.

Baldwin refers to this in *The Fire Next Time* and elsewhere when he speaks of white people being trapped in their own histories—histories that end up ensnaring all of us because of bad art and harmful myths. What we need, as Baldwin understood, is art that opens our eyes—all of our eyes—and serves as a corrective for exclusion and derision. As I've written elsewhere, deliberately echoing Baldwin, "Tearing down the racial mythologies that keep us separate and locked in our own distinct prisons will lead to liberation for all of us."[38]

Bad art cannot serve as a witness to the reality of what is happening in a culture because it confirms the presuppositions of an audience or consoles them into thinking that the cracks in the veneer are merely cosmetic. Bad art does not trust people to accompany it into difficult territory for art and story's sake, but tries to cajole and entice them along—or to offer them a soothing anesthetic. Baldwin cites T. S. Eliot's remark that people cannot bear very much reality, another iteration of Socrates's theory of the unexamined life. It is easier to look away, or to see badly, than to reckon with a world of others sunk in suffering, particularly when you and people like you bear responsibility for that state of the world.

That evasion is especially damaging if you are one of those outsiders who is misrepresented. "For a person to bear his life, he needs a valid re-creation of that life," Baldwin says. Barry Jenkins, who directed *Moonlight* (2016) and the film version of Baldwin's *If Beale Street Could Talk* (2018), similarly notes that if you are not represented in the art you encounter, it is as if you don't exist: "When you have such a lack of representation, such a lack of images, two things can happen. Either you start to feel like you're voiceless, or people who don't live in close proximity to you can conveniently start to think you don't exist, that you're invisible. When images do arise to fill that lack, they take on added importance."[39]

Artistic lack of representation is equally damaging to those who don't live in close proximity to different experiences, whose eyes can remain closed to the diversity and challenge of lives not their own (that willful delusion of which Baldwin spoke). When Baldwin writes about the lies and evasions of Hollywood films, he is recognizing how art can reinforce a shuttered view of reality rather than witnessing to an expanded vision, can let its largely white consumers off the hook rather than bracing them with the truth about a larger world. Too much American art is escapist, either consciously or unconsciously; in a sense, it is the precise opposite of the jeremiad that demands honest engagement.

So it is that Baldwin writes of a "race film" like *The Defiant Ones* (1958), starring Tony Curtis and the great Sidney Poitier, two escaped inmates shackled together who are trying to reach freedom, that it is a movie "with people we are accustomed to seeing in the movies," but that it sugarcoats its message of racial tolerance and that even "the unmistakable truth" of Poitier's performance is placed in the service of a lie.[40] The shackled prisoners are represented as hating each other, but the film ignores a very simple truth, as Baldwin sees it: "Black men do not have the same reason to hate white men as white men have to hate blacks." White men hate Black people, he says, because of terror and dread, because of the myths they have created and spread that Black people are dangerous and subhuman. "But the root of the black man's hatred is rage, and he does not so much hate white men as simply want them out of his way, and more than that, out of his children's way."[41] Simply put, whites hate Blacks because they fear what Black people could do to them; Blacks hate whites because of what white people have done to them. It is not in any way the same, and the fears of white audiences are imaginary, despite all the damage those fears have caused and continue to cause.

White critics approached *The Defiant Ones* through their own filters. Bosley Crowther of the *New York Times* saw the thoughtful and challenging film he hoped to see about the egalitarian society in which he wanted to live: "These two men, who think they are so profoundly different, are in basic respects the same. Each is the victim of cruel oppressions, each has his hopes and dreams, and each, as a consequence of frustrations, has committed crime." Crowther's sense of the movie's conclusion is that it demonstrates "their complete commonality. In the end, it is clear that they are brothers, stripped of all vulgar bigotry."[42] But these characters do not occupy equal worlds, nor is their understanding of each other's humanity the same, even though the film chooses to imagine they are equally yoked because they are shackled together, just as white and Black people in this country are imprisoned in our common history.

When, at film's end, Poitier's Noah jumps off the train rather than abandon Curtis's Joker, white audiences cheered and still cheer; it is, to them, a gesture of brotherhood, of Black nobility, and of forgiveness. These two men have moved from hatred to love or, at least, to an acceptance that allows white audiences to feel good about themselves and to imagine possibilities for racial reconciliation despite the fact that the film itself suggests that social conditions and prejudices have not changed in the slightest.

Black audiences, meanwhile, Baldwin says, see that same scene as ridiculous and completely untrue to the experiences of a Black man in America. "The Harlem audience," he says of the screening he attended, "was outraged, and yelled, *Get back on the train, you fool!*"[43]

Like a multitude of later race-reconciliation movies including Academy Award–winners *Driving Miss Daisy* (1989) and *Green Book* (2018), both of which I suspect Baldwin would have derided, *The Defiant Ones* twists the truth about race, power, and even what it means to be a man in America in order to salve the consciences of its white audiences. Although it purports to address America and its racial divide, it does not tell the truth about America or the racial divide, and so it cannot bear faithful witness.

Another popular movie, *In the Heat of the Night*, despite some radical scenes for its 1967 year of release, also, Baldwin argues, evades and dismisses the issues of race and injustice that the film "imagines itself to be about."[44] It is about the altered racial understanding of a single white person, in this case a small-town Mississippi lawman, Sheriff Gillespie (played by Rod Steiger). Gillespie initially arrests the Philadelphia police detective Virgil Tibbs (Poitier, again, in another movie he elevates) as a murder suspect, then works alongside him to solve the crime. It becomes clear during the course of the story that Gillespie, who is an ardent racist, develops a deep respect for Tibbs who is, by a factor of ten, the smartest person in the movie.

At the end of *In the Heat of the Night*, all crimes solved, Gillespie takes Tibbs to catch the train, even carrying his bag, and there is a moment of connection between them. Baldwin says that in a typical Hollywood love story, this would be the moment for "the kiss." In 1967, of course, a white man and a Black man in a Hollywood film were not going to kiss at the train station, but Baldwin is correct: it is a dramatic moment acknowledging their common humanity and a recognition of the respect that Sheriff Gillespie has developed for Virgil Tibbs.

The obligatory fade-out kiss in American movies, Baldwin notes, is not about love, or even less about sex: "It spoke about all things now becoming possible. It was a device desperately needed among a people for whom so much had to be made possible."[45] Like the gesture of Poitier leaping off the train rather than leave Tony Curtis behind, it is a moment of connection between two characters that allows audiences to ignore the many larger problems that remain unsolved, and largely unacknowledged, despite the good intentions of their liberal white filmmakers.

None of this is remarkable, nor is it limited to art, fiction, and stories from America. In a generic comedy (by which I mean a story that may or may not contain humor, but which ends with a kiss or a wedding signaling that society will continue, and that these individual characters will survive or even thrive), the closing symbols often struggle mightily against the weight of the larger story that precedes it. In William Shakespeare's *Much Ado about Nothing*, for example, while multiple hearts have been broken, many harmful things said, and a multitude of skeletons have been flung out of closets, all is papered over by two promised weddings and a closing dance. The failure of *In the Heat of the Night* for Baldwin is that it tries to do too much too quickly, disregards or ignores so much to reach its ending, desirable as that ending might be. While Baldwin gives those who made the film credit for making it—one must at least acknowledge that the hearts of writers of protest literature are in the right place—it simply does not succeed. The movie, he says,

> helplessly conveys—without confronting—the anguish of people trapped in a legend. They cannot live within this legend. Neither can they step out of it....

> The history which produces such a film cannot, after all, be swiftly understood, or can the effects of this history be easily resolved. . . . Virgil Tibbs goes back to where they call him *Mister* . . . and the sheriff has gone back to the niggers, who are really his only assignment. And nothing, alas, has been made possible by this obligatory, fade-out kiss, this preposterous adventure: except that white Americans have been encouraged to continue dreaming, and black Americans have been alerted to the necessity of waking up.[46]

The art that tells the truth in all of these movies is not the stories, all of them written and directed by white men. Where these movies tell truth and honestly challenge their cultures is primarily in the performances by Poitier. Theologian Kelly Brown Douglas has said on multiple occasions that whatever the truth or falsehood of the movies he inhabited, the larger-than-life truth of the actor Sidney Poitier simply could not be denied. He was the first Black man she ever saw on a movie screen, and he represented the strong, smart, beautiful Black men of her own experience. *New York Times* film critic Wesley Morris, writing on the occasion of Poitier's death in 2022, notes how before Poitier's movies, "Black characters were jolly statuary—hoisting luggage, serving food, tending children—meant to decorate a white American's dream." Poitier, was, he said, America's greatest movie star. Not the greatest Black movie star. The greatest of all time, period. Few actors have ever carried so much weight in appearing onscreen, and Poitier did so nobly.[47]

I said something similar in my own remembrance of Sir Sidney:

> The lives he embodied demonstrated strength, intelligence, dignity and the sacred possibility of connection.

Virgil Tibbs could develop a friendship with a bigoted white sheriff, and teacher Mark Thackeray in *To Sir, with Love* could advocate for the humanity of his inner-city students because—although Poitier would not have said so in such theological language—he could recognize in them fellow children of God, just as his very human presence allowed them to make that same connection.

In the Heat of the Night, for example, contains a scene that Baldwin describes in detail in *The Devil Finds Work*, a gasp-worthy moment in 1967. Chief Gillespie and Detective Tibbs go to visit the most prominent white man in town, whom we might identify as the plantation owner, a decadent rich racist who is breeding orchids in a hothouse straight out of Hollywood central casting. When he realizes that Tibbs is actually interrogating him for the murder, he is outraged. He slaps Virgil Tibbs, and Tibbs slaps him back. In 1967, a primarily white audience would have sat there, their eyes wide, because this is a Black power moment. The slap was not in the script, but Poitier insisted that it be added, since as I have written, "Always conscious that he represented millions of people every time he acted, he could not allow his character to accept attacks on his humanity without a response."[48]

Poitier was a hero of the civil rights movement. He embodied moments in mainstream Hollywood films when a Black character says, *I will not allow you to treat me in this way anymore. You do not have the right to direct violence at me.* A sign carried at many of the civil rights protests in the 1960s read, "I am a man," and that is what Poitier insisted with his humanity and equality in performances that showed him as a human blessed with intelligence, strength, and dignity. He was the kind of performer Baldwin wrote for: in his casting notes for his dramatic writing, he leaned toward great actors like Poitier, who was originally supposed to star on Broadway in Baldwin's *Blues for Mister Charlie.*

Art that honestly reflects a culture does not have to be unrelievedly noble, nor should it depict characters of color, or outside the white Christian mainstream, as perfect. Remember Baldwin's criticism of *Guess Who's Coming to Dinner*'s Wonder Doctor as an example of a character who never could or should exist. Baldwin himself wrote characters who were simultaneously flawed and noble and true. In *If Beale Street Could Talk*, for example, it is clear that the Black characters swim upstream in a society that makes every aspect of their life more challenging. Tish talks, for example, about the experience of going to visit Fonny in jail and how it brings front and center all of the hard truths about life for the marginalized in America.

If bad art lies about the culture, minimizes or glosses over hard truths; if protest literature focuses on issues to the detriment of its characters; then Baldwin argues that great art tells the truth, the whole truth. In *If Beale Street Could Talk*, there are Black characters who are ignoble or simply irritating. Despite a world shaped by white prejudice, they may indulge their own prejudices. Fonny's mother, Mrs. Hunt, is fair-skinned, and so she doesn't believe that Tish ("I'm dark and my hair is plain hair and there is nothing very outstanding about me") is good enough for her son. As Tish says, Mrs. Hunt and her daughters "are fair; and you could see that Mrs. Hunt had been a very beautiful girl down there in Atlanta.... And she still had—has—that look, that don't touch me look, that women who were beautiful carry with them to the grave."[49]

Among many instances of unconditional love represented in this community of those who suffered is the scene when Tish tells her family that she is carrying Fonny's baby, although Fonny is in jail, and they are not yet married. Her mother tells her how when enslaved people were brought to America, the white man "didn't give us no preachers to say words over us before we had our babies." She tells Tish that there is nothing to be ashamed of, that the baby will be loved and a source of joy, and that Fonny will need the baby to have strength and courage to endure jail.[50] At dinner, she invites Tish's father to pour from the last bottle of the good brandy. "This is sacrament," she tells them at the table. "We're drinking to a new life. Tish is going to have Fonny's baby." They raise their glasses. It could have been a moment of shame and regret—nothing is going to be easy about this baby or this baby's life—but Baldwin captures instead this moment of unconditional love and total acceptance. "It is a miracle," Tish says, "to realize that somebody loves you."[51]

Baldwin's purpose is not simply to talk about how difficult the world is for Black people; it is to depict his characters living in the real world with all the reactions that real people have: anger and sadness and bitterness, infighting and attempts to impose internal hierarchies over money or social status or gradations of skin color or religion or occupation, despair and lament, but also tiny human victories of love and life, of dignity, of thoughts and dreams that can't be taken away.

If good art depicts society critically and honestly, it can and should also depict its characters as fully rounded and capable of the full range of human emotions, no matter what their social circumstances. Baldwin, who railed against the necessity for Poitier to play a hyper-qualified Wonder Doctor in *Guess Who's Coming to Dinner* also railed against the diminished and reductive Black characters of Bigger Thomas and Uncle Tom in literature, of Stepin Fetchit and Mammy characters in the American cinema.

Finally, Baldwin believed that bad art left humans mired in themselves while great art lifted them out of themselves and exalted them, connected them to others, and perhaps even to something greater than themselves, whatever that force might be. Remember Barry Jenkins (who directed *Moonlight* and the film version of Baldwin's *If Beale Street Could Talk*) and his comments on representation, on how a story needs to show people to themselves. As Jenkins says in another interview, "If you don't give people a productive, honest, organic image of their lives, they're going to start to think they don't exist. I think there's a space to be filled."[52]

Art tells us something about ourselves, about what we need to overcome, and about what we can aspire to be. Sometimes it tells us things we don't know—or don't want to know, things we haven't seen or understood about the world or about ourselves. In his lengthy interview with the *Paris Review*, Baldwin retold a story of walking through New York City with his painter mentor Beauford Delaney:

> I remember standing on a street corner with the black painter Beauford Delaney down in the Village, waiting for the light to change, and he pointed down and said, "Look." I looked and all I saw was water. And he said, "Look again," which I did, and I saw oil on the water and the city reflected in the puddle. It was a great revelation to me. I can't explain it. He taught me how to see, and how to trust what I saw. Painters have often taught writers how to see. And once you've had that experience, you see differently.[53]

Making art is about helping yourself and those who consume your art see. I often learn about the world and myself in the process of writing fiction, and my most valued communications come from readers who say my work has helped them see something about themselves and the world. Baldwin described his art in terms of learning, of having the courage to accept the things we don't know: "The whole language of writing for me is finding out what you don't want to know, what you don't want to find out."[54]

We'll be exploring what those things might be, how Baldwin writes about faith, about politics, about courage, about understanding who we are and who we are meant to be. But suffice it to say this: while he would confess that great art should hold our interest, what separates good art from unsuccessful art is that it also teaches us something about the world and ourselves. It challenges us. It moves us to a new place.

At different stages of our lives we may see ourselves reflected anew. For instance, I've been reading Ernest Hemingway's *The Sun Also Rises* and Ernest Gaines's *A Lesson before Dying*, and watching Spike Lee's *Do the Right Thing*, at least once a year for the past thirty years, and every time I lean into these works, I learn something about what it means to be human, about how I am supposed to live, about how I am supposed to die, about what truly matters. I don't experience them today as I did in my twenties.

Baldwin tells a story about a dinner with his friend who stepped off the George Washington Bridge to his death, the incident that at least partly caused Baldwin to flee America lest he end up following in his friend's footsteps. They argued about the state of the world and Baldwin told him that people are awful, that they don't want to be better, and what are you going to do about that? Baldwin's friend looked at him and asked, "What about love?"

"You'd better forget about that, my friend," Baldwin says he told him. "That train has *gone*."

Baldwin regretted saying this, even more so when his friend looked back across the table at him and said, "You're a poet . . . and you don't believe in love," and then laid his head down to cry.

They both believed in the importance and usefulness of art, and the valuable role of the artist. But Baldwin felt he had betrayed those things, that he was wrong. "My unexamined life would not allow me to speak otherwise," he tells us.[55] Later, he knew better, his hope returning to fuel his art, when he says, "The war of an artist with his society is a lover's war, and he does, at his best, what lovers do, which is to reveal the beloved to himself, and with the revelation, make freedom real."[56] Great art calls a society to something better, reveals it and its people, and gives them insights they never could have had from mere entertainment.

Baldwin's work shows our selves to ourselves and invites us to respond. And as we move forward in this conversation, we'll see how that invitation is presented, and how we might react to it. Art can help us grapple with issues of race and faith and identity—all of the big questions, really. And Mr. Baldwin was there before us, will be there after us, and he can help us embrace our own questions and see some possible solutions to them.

Baldwin on Faith

Something active, something more like a fire,
like the wind, something which can
change you.... I mean a passionate belief, a pas-
sionate knowledge of what a human
being can do, and become, what a human
being can do to change the world.

—James Baldwin, 1965

On a warm, sunny day in Paris in 2022, I sat down in the Parc Monceau with a book of James Baldwin interviews. On a slatted wooden bench, the sun in my eyes, my journal open and ready for notes, I read. In a 1965 interview, Baldwin was asked about Malcolm X; the Nation of Islam, with which Malcolm was connected; and the philosophy of white hatred Malcolm espoused. Baldwin was crystal clear about his feelings, saying that he would "much rather die than become that kind of theologian."[1]

It was a significant phrase from a person so careful with words, and an odd choice to name himself in such a way.

I serve as the canon theologian at the American Cathedral in Paris, and so I can tell you that I am often asked what, exactly, such a designation means. Simply put, a theologian is a person who attempts to talk about God, and theologians are people who reflect on God, faith communities, salvation, justice, the future, and the truth from within a certain religious or wisdom tradition. So: I do Christian theology. Others might do Jewish theology or Muslim theology or Shinto theology. When Baldwin spoke of himself as being one sort of theologian in opposition to another represented by the early Malcolm X, he was claiming a certain vision of God, faith, and life—and also proclaiming that he *had* a certain vision of God, faith, and life.

He was saying that despite all the ways he might have turned his back formally on the American church, there was still something meaningful about the life of faith that compelled his attention, and perhaps even his faithfulness.

When I preached about James Baldwin on All Saints Sunday at Wilshire Baptist Church in Dallas, Texas, later that year, I put it like this: "If he were standing here today, I like to think that the people of Wilshire Baptist Church would recognize and honor that spark of Jesus within James Baldwin that never went out."[2]

As we noted earlier, Baldwin was deeply religious during his youth. Like his parents, he was immersed in the Black church, and like his stepfather David—the only father he ever knew—Baldwin was a Christian preacher. Ayana Mathis notes that "Baldwin was himself raised in the Pentecostal faith and was a preacher until the age of 17, when he left the church to become the man he was destined to be."[3] By all accounts, Baldwin was an exciting, inspired, and gifted minister of the Christian faith, albeit within the context of a sin and salvation gospel and a racially constricted understanding of how God was and was not moving in the world and in American society.

Baldwin left that church—and, he believed, the larger church—for reasons he spent his career enumerating, many of which we explore here.

In an interview with the *New York Times* in 1963—prior to that 1965 identification of himself as a certain kind of theologian—he explained that (as the *Times* headed the section) he was "Not a Churchgoer," but said there were clearly ways in which the church continued to work in his heart and life. "Every artist," he told the *Times*, "is fundamentally religious.... I haven't been in a church for twenty years. Nevertheless, when [William] Blake talks about the New Jerusalem, I believe."[4]

As with all the topics explored in this book, James Baldwin proves himself to be a thoughtful guide who has something to teach us about faith and practice if we are willing to pay attention. While he left the church, while he constantly identified himself as a person outside any formal tradition of Christianity, he continued to use the language of church, the Bible, and theology.

In 1970 Baldwin told interviewer John Hall that the three formative influences on his life and work were "my father, the Church, and Charles Dickens."[5] In 1979 Baldwin argued to Kalamu ya Salaam that everything in Black history comes out of the church, that what Black people did with the Bible and the Cross was nothing less than astounding.[6] And in 1984, just a few years before his death, he said to Black civil rights activist and professor Julius Lester, "I am a witness. In the church in which I was raised, you were supposed to bear witness to the truth."[7] He never stopped speaking out of that heritage; as the young Black woman Ida discovers in the novel *Another Country* (1962), once you have religion, you never really lose it: "It's funny, I haven't thought about church or any of that type stuff for years. But it's still there.... Nothing ever goes away."[8]

So on the one hand, like many Americans (and like me, raised to be devoutly Southern Baptist, who then spent twenty-five years outside that or any faith), Baldwin fled the church, and in his public utterances said that he had never gone back. He very consciously and vocally told the world that he could not be a Christian, because the Christian church as he had observed it had failed to live out its message. But in his literary and public utterances, he also continued to speak the language of the church, to reflect the many ways that the King James translation of the Bible had seeped into his blood and into his bones, to echo religious ways of thinking about the world. Houston minister Ralph Douglas West—considered one of the best preachers in the world—told me that there was no question in his mind that Baldwin remained a preacher to the end of his life.

When I looked through Baldwin's letters to his literary executor Robert Park Mills, I was surprised—and then not surprised—to find that on numerous occasions Baldwin wrote to Mills detailing his professional, emotional, and spiritual struggles, and ended by asking Mills, "Pray for me." To see, in a November 1961 letter from Turkey, Baldwin saying about his work on the essay "Down at the Cross," "It's my hope that God will be good and that it won't take too long to hammer into its final shape." To read a letter from Jerusalem, where Baldwin was writing from the Upper Room, "the room where Christ and his disciples had the last supper, and I thought on Mahalia [Jackson] and Marian [Anderson] and *Go Down, Moses* and of my father and of that song my father loved to sing, *I want to be ready to walk in Jerusalem, just like John.*"[9]

To hear Baldwin throughout his life—including in the play left unfinished at his death—speak about the Christian concept of the Welcome Table, a place where all would be respected, loved, seen, known, and fed. To hear Baldwin model being

some kind of theologian in response to life's big personal and
political questions. To hear the recording of Baldwin singing
(accompanied only by simple gospel piano) his favorite hymn,
"Precious Lord, Take My Hand," at the celebration of his life
held at St. John the Divine Cathedral in New York City:

> *Precious Lord, take my hand*
> *Lead me on, let me stand*
> *I am tired, I am weak, I am worn*
> *Through the storm, through the night*
> *Lead me on to the light*
> *Precious Lord, take my hand, lead me home.*[10]

Like many people I know (and indeed, like my younger
self), Baldwin rebelled against the strictures and structures of
the church in which he was raised, finding them untenable
or even soul-killing. At the same time, it became clear that he
saw some continuing value in understanding himself within a
Christian framework, that he never stopped recognizing himself as a person somehow steeped in faith. Raise up a child in
the way that he should go, the Good Book says (and Baldwin
repeats in *The Amen Corner*), and when he is grown, he will not
depart from it.[11] In his explanation for rejecting the Nation of
Islam in *The Fire Next Time*, Baldwin makes clear that despite
their Muslim trappings, the organization feels too much like
the Christianity he left; what he is suspicious of is dogmatism
in any faith, particularly views of one's own rightness and fitness
that lead inexorably to hatred and violence, whether those views
are espoused by white Christians or by Black Muslims.

Baldwin spent his adult life consciously separating himself
from institutional Christianity. He witnessed the ways that both
the white church and the Black church failed the faithful and

the world. As Baldwin said on *The Dick Cavett Show*, it meant that he couldn't afford to trust most white Christians, or to trust the Christian church, which, as he says in *No Name in the Street*, "has betrayed and dishonored [their] Savior.... The Christians do not believe in their Savior (who has certainly failed to save them)."[12] But given the many religious references and symbols in his work, given the rhetorical flourishes and the Christian epigraphs, Baldwin seems to embody Paul Thomas Anderson's line from *Magnolia* (1999), a powerful film about alienated and broken people: "We may be through with the past, but the past is not through with us."

For those who think of Baldwin as outside the Christian tradition, it's useful to reflect not just on his uses of the tradition but on the ways that people within it understood and recognized him. Dr. Martin Luther King Jr.'s lawyer Clarence B. Jones wrote to Baldwin's literary agent Bob Mills about the groundbreaking *New Yorker* essay "A Letter from a Region in My Mind" (later "Down at the Cross" in *The Fire Next Time*). Jones said he had asked King about those who called Baldwin's essay "anti-Christian," and that King had completely rejected that characterization. "Not only does Dr. King not regard it as such," Jones said, "but on the contrary regards it, as so many other people do, as one of the most brilliant statements of American race relations that has been written."[13] Other Christian leaders also heard Baldwin's hard but honest assessment of religion and race with sympathy. Nicholas Buccola described how a Methodist minister wrote to the *New Yorker* to communicate this: Mr. Baldwin might have left the church, he said, but "Down at the Cross" "was one of the most profoundly Christian things that I ever read."[14]

Many Christians look at Baldwin's books not as works by an alien outsider but by a fellow traveler. Danté Stewart, in his memoir *Shoutin' in the Fire*, wrote about how King and Baldwin, James Cone and Toni Morrison, Fannie Lou Hamer and Malcolm X might have lost faith, but "never in themselves, in what could be true of God, and true in the struggle." So it was, Stewart writes, that we can see ourselves, "Like James Baldwin … holding on to Jesus while also living with our fear, trauma, doubts, and hopes. Our story and the story of Jesus are bound together in faith, hope, love, and community."[15]

Baldwin understands what it means to honestly think of oneself as Christian—and how that identity should genuinely challenge and complicate our lives and our national identity.

What Baldwin believes about faith, I would argue, is that belief and action badly applied make us more dangerous, more limited, more blinkered in our vision. A bad religious understanding may breed jealousy, greed, and hatred. Bad faith may in fact be worse than no faith at all. But rightly applied, faith and hope make us bigger, better human beings, capable of seeing and loving the world and all those in it, capable of working for larger aims than our own desires, capable of living in hope rather than in fear. Baldwin argued late in life, "I know that we can be better than we are."[16] It was, he said, the limit of his wisdom.

But it is indeed wisdom. Baldwin's life and consideration of the vocation of theologian—that is, to ask, *Who is God, who am I, what is sacred community, how are we supposed to live, why exercise faith?*—allow us to benefit from that wisdom, to see why faith and faith communities are necessary, to condemn and turn away from spiritual practices that are divisive and soul killing, and to embrace a religious and spiritual tradition that calls us to be better than we are—to embrace the vocation to which we are called: to bear witness to the truth.

So what is religion for? Plenty of people around the world think of religion as, at best, unnecessary, and at worst backward or dangerous. Bad applications of religion can lead to violence like the 9/11 attacks or the rise of white Christian nationalism. Charles Kimball has said that when we are absolutely certain we are in the right, we find ourselves in a dangerous place: "Blind obedience to individuals or to doctrines," he argues, "is never wise." Absolute certainty and exclusion of those who don't see the world precisely as we do can tend to lead us to perform evil acts, even in the name of sincere religious beliefs, since "people armed with absolute truth claims are closely linked to violent extremism, charismatic leaders, and various justifications for acts otherwise understood to be unacceptable."[17] But faith or wisdom traditions also fill a multitude of human needs for us as they help us find useful answers to a variety of existential questions: *Who and what is God? How are we supposed to worship, serve, seek this God? How are we supposed to live with each other? What can give my life meaning? What is meaning? How can I recognize a wisdom or faith tradition that might be dangerous or deadly to me?*

Where could I find a vision of God and of Beloved Community that might save my life?

That last is by no means least. Many of us come to faith after other things have failed us—maybe after everything else has failed. We ask God to be present, somehow, when we find ourselves at our most vulnerable, our most broken, our most lost. The reality that James Baldwin wrote about in his stories and essays included his own very real suffering—and that of all people. He knew what it was to face alienation and despair. On more than one occasion, he gave thought to taking his own life. As we have heard, one of Baldwin's dearest friends, Eugene Worth, died by suicide after jumping from the George Washington Bridge. Baldwin's biographer David Leeming notes that "Baldwin feared a similar fate," and part of his flight to Paris was an attempt to escape this, although the loneliness and pain were in some ways always with him.[18] In a letter to his brother David about his trip to Istanbul in 1965, Baldwin wrote that the seas were rough, as they always are for the lonely long-distance swimmer.[19] For all his friends, lovers, and admirers, despite a life in which he was lionized and extolled, Baldwin still knew what it was to feel lost and alone.

My student Daniel Smith, after rereading Baldwin's major works, wrote me this:

> It may not even be a stretch to claim that alienation is Baldwin's central preoccupation, the operative lens through which he conducts his commentary on race, theology, literature, history, culture, love, hate, and identity.... Baldwin's exile is not my exile, but his efforts to sketch his relationship to the state of exile resonate with me viscerally; that the conclusions of his lonely journey are grounded in hope, love, and self-empowerment is nothing short of miraculous, to me.[20]

So, again, why do we need religion? What is the importance of God? Some of us would have to say that we need to believe in a power larger than ourselves because left to ourselves we are doomed, damned, in desperate need of rescue, and well aware that we cannot effect that rescue through any means known to us. Hope, love, and self-empowerment do not seem possible.

In Christian understandings, the word "lost" is used to describe this feeling, although lostness is a universal concept. In "Amazing Grace," one of our foundational hymns, we hear, "I once was lost, but now am found." In evangelical Christian salvation teachings, those who have not believed in Jesus as their personal savior are said to be lost and doomed to eternal hellfire.

(Baldwin writes in *The Fire Next Time* that when he found religion in the Black church, he "discovered God, His saints and angels, and His blazing Hell.")[21] While this is a powerful and frightening teaching, this aspect of lostness did not speak to Baldwin, nor does it encourage many of us. But we do understand what it feels like to be lost.

In the church of my youth, I was taught that being lost and separated from God was strictly about my sinfulness, which was terrifying. But being lost may be less about personal morality and more about the universal human condition.

"I was lost, but now am found. Was blind, but now I see."

Protestant Christian theologian Paul Tillich spoke of sin in a way which I have always found edifying, and I believe could speak into Baldwin's understanding of God, the universe, and everything. Tillich thought of sin in terms of separation: what we might call sin is anything that separates me from God, from my neighbor, and from myself.[22] When I sin, I act in a way that distances me from the creator, from those around me, and from my own best self. A definition of lostness is compelling, for it explains so much about how we alienate ourselves from things that truly matter, and in Baldwin's writing we can see that reflected. Human brokenness is, naturally enough, one of the most important concepts that Baldwin is trying to understand and ameliorate. In his novel *Another Country*, the "emptiness and horror" of this lostness is reflected in the words of the blues singer Bessie Smith: "There's thousands of people ain't got no place to go."[23]

As the novel begins, Rufus has suffered a grievous personal loss and is separated from his family, from the faith community of his family, from friends and meaningful work, from justice and the divine. He is profoundly alone, in the horrific position of having to sell his body—again—to feed himself, and he recognizes that doing this one more time might be the death of him. He prays, "I've got so little left, Lord, don't let me lose it all."[24]

Throughout *Another Country*, the continuing refrain "You ain't got to be afraid" echoes; the soul-killing nature of fear is explored.[25] Fear can keep us from loving and risking; it is in itself a kind of death. This is an essential spiritual lesson. Throughout the Bible, Old and New Testaments alike, we find passages instructing believers not to be afraid. I am drawn to Isaiah 41:10: "Do not fear, for I am with you, do not be afraid, for I am your God; I will strengthen you, I will help you, I will uphold you with my victorious right hand."[26] In the Christian Gospels, Jesus admonishes people not to be afraid. One of my favorite instances is in the Gospel of Mark when a religious leader, Jairus, comes to Jesus to beg him to heal his daughter who is desperately ill. Before they can reach the house, friends come to tell them that Jairus's daughter has died, that there's no need for the Teacher to travel any further. Jesus simply turns to Jairus and says, "Don't be afraid. Just believe."[27] Clearly, looking at the many times Jesus utters the phrase "Fear not," it represents one of his central spiritual teachings. In life—or faced with death—we are not to be afraid.

It's sad and startling to see so many people today living in the framework of Christian belief through a filter of fear: *I'm afraid of people who don't look like us, who don't believe like us, of anything I don't understand, of what I can't know.* As Jesus's repeated words suggest, fear is distinctly unchristian, and Baldwin argues in conjunction with faith, with justice, and with human life in general that we are called to live and love valiantly and without fear, however frightening the world may be.

The roll call of Baldwin characters who are at least initially broken and lost in spiritual and emotional senses is massive and global. It is Baldwin himself in essays and letters; it is Baldwin's father, David, who "had a terrible life; he was defeated long before he died"); it is Malcolm Little / Malcolm X, imprisoned literally and figuratively, and others he sees who are "aimless, lost, without hope" in *One Day When I Was Lost* (1972); it is both Richard and Parnell in *Blues for Mister Charlie* (1964); it is David in *Giovanni's Room*; it is Leo in *Tell Me How Long the Train's Been Gone* (1968); it is many of the characters in "Sonny's Blues," but particularly Sonny, wrestling with addiction; it is Leona and Cass and Richard and Eric in *Another Country*, as well, of course, as Rufus.[28]

Religion and practice can provide meaning and healing to the brokenhearted, can give shape and form to lives limned by chaos, can offer encouragement or even a chance to climb out of those deep, dark holes where many of us—and many of Baldwin's characters—have been or still are. Early in *Go Tell It on the Mountain*, John Grimes witnesses the opening moments of worship at the Temple of the Fire Baptized: how those parishioners "sang with all the strength that was in them, and clapped their hands for joy.... Their singing caused him to believe in the presence of the Lord; indeed, it was no longer a question of belief, because they made that presence real."[29] When Malcolm Little / Malcolm X embraces even the bastardized Islam of the Nation of Islam, he finds purpose: "God is great. I know there's love and hope.... We can change."[30] My own life—and the lives of many of us who have come or come back to faith—have been saved and enriched by religion. But it is possible for religion to become harmful, despite the community and comfort it can provide.

Baldwin wrote that, as a young man, he was at the church in Harlem seeking safety from "the evil within me and the evil without."[31] Baldwin looked around at those he knew in Harlem and saw that all responded to fear and suffering somehow:

"Some went on wine or whiskey or the needle, and are still on it. And others, like me, fled into the church."[32] His first faith experience offered a way of being and a way of seeing the world, although it was ultimately not redemptive for him.

He grew up in a tradition familiar to many conservative American Christians. In that tradition, religion is defined by emotion, by narrow moralities and sureties: one comes to God on God's terms, accepts a set of defined faith statements, rejects a multitude of cultural complications, and tries to live as a holy person in an unholy world. Once saved, a true Christian has to hold tightly to faith no matter what happens, and to let go of the old self and put away the old sins.

Our church traditions counted a number of so-called vices that both Baldwin and I ended up finding meaningful and even sacramental: drinking, smoking, dancing and secular music, bars, movies, the human body. Baldwin's lawyers prepared for him a 1962 budget that actually featured a line item titled "Spirits for Creativity (wines and liquors)"; while working on this book, I have more than once had a glass of something on hand, or celebrated a good hard day's writing with a Manhattan. I daresay we have both been decent people despite how the churches of our youth might react to these declarations.[33]

Rules can be a comfort; there's a reason why so many American Christians give more credence to what they perceive to be the Apostle Paul's easy formulas for salvation than they do to Jesus's often cryptic stories and teachings. And I remember as a young man feeling proud (over-proud) that I was part of a holy community trying to live with integrity and morality. Although it was a long way from the Harlem he wrote about, I had intimate experience of the world Baldwin described in *Go Tell It on the Mountain*. That was my childhood and teen years in the Southern Baptist tradition. Never holy enough. Always afraid of hellfire and brimstone. Suspicious of the world around us. But also surrounded by people who were creating a common story about God and how we related to God that gave many of us real comfort. See, for example, many of the characters in Baldwin's play *The Amen Corner*, called to live by perhaps unrealistic standards of piety, or Mrs. Hunt from *If Beale Street Could Talk*, so blinded by what she believes to be the immorality of the baby that her son Fonny and Tish have made that she curses that child in Tish's womb. It could be and often was a painful faith, but it also created meaning, of a sort. The question was whether that meaning was worth keeping, or if it might in its own way be soul-killing.

Baldwin saw the church of his childhood operating as one of two poles in the Black community. In the broken world permitted by white supremacy, you could give yourself up to sin and sorrow—to drugs and prostitution, drinking and despair—or you could give yourself to God and hope for release in the world to come. Ayana Mathis saw this in Baldwin's experience and her own: "Church was a place where Black people could speak their pain or their rage, free of the endless and violent scrutiny of whiteness. It was a place we could be ourselves; a place to be joyful and a place to mourn."[34] Still, it is no surprise that although Baldwin excelled as a preacher in this culture, he saw through the cracks in the veneer, and spoke and wrote about them.

He saw the painful irony of the suffering Christ being used to hold suffering people in check, of Christianity being used as a mechanism of control and anesthesia, or even of class warfare within the Black community. He also saw the larger American church failing to stand for the values for which its founder lived and died and rose again. I have heard Kelly Brown Douglas say that slaveholders may have introduced enslaved people to Christianity, but they did not introduce them to the liberating God.

Baldwin would agree; Christianity was a vehicle for white power and control, not for Black liberation. "The Christian church," as Baldwin wrote in 1972, "has betrayed and dishonored and blasphemed that Savior in whose name they have slaughtered millions and millions and millions of people. And if this mighty objection seems trivial, it can only be because of the total hardening of the heart and the coarsening of the conscience among those people who believed that their power has given them the exclusive right to history."[35]

Black theology developed as a response to white Christianity, for the suffering Christ seemed to have more in common with the marginalized than with the ruling classes. James Cone, the founder of Black liberation theology, made this comparison explicit in his book *The Cross and the Lynching Tree*, in which the spectacles of public crucifixion and public lynching are found to be analogous: "Until we can see the cross and the lynching tree together, until we can identify Christ with a 'recrucified' black body hanging from a lynching tree, there can be no genuine understanding of Christian identity in America, and no deliverance from the brutal legacy of slavery and white supremacy."[36] Likewise my friend and Oxford theologian Anthony Reddie said that Black theology had to be understood in response to "its relationship to the experience of oppression of Black people in the world."[37]

Still, while the Black church could be (and has been) involved in the real liberation of lives as well as souls, it is still related to the Church Universal long controlled by white people. Baldwin did not have the benefit of reading James H. Cone or Kelly Brown Douglas for a Black take on a truly liberating Christianity. This brings to mind Frederick Douglass, who spoke of two churches, one spiritual and holy, one political and repressive. This latter slaveholding Christianity, he wrote, is what he condemned in his *Autobiography,* not some true

Christianity with Christ at its center.[38] It was that latter church that he and Baldwin and many others have called to task over the centuries, a church tied into the everyday repression of Black people and many others. Even the Black Church had its problems, its injustices, and its hypocrisies—hence his teenage flight from it.

Was Christianity a freeing force, an enslaving force, or an excruciatingly painful combination of the two? Baldwin, I think, would have landed on the last. In his lifelong love of Black Gospel, for example, often used as epigraphs in his work, he found a comforting message and a liberating energy. In the discipline and moral teachings of the faith there was some value, especially compared to the destructive downward spiral of drugs, drink, violence, and prostitution that Baldwin witnessed in Harlem. But American Christianity was both a comfort and a curse. Baldwin believed that despite the Blackness of his church, God remained white, the God of white people, and Jesus was and still is often depicted as white despite his earthly incarnation as a brown-skinned Palestinian peasant.

Malcolm X argues against this oppressive image in the Baldwin screenplay *One Day When I Was Lost.* He confronts a Bible teacher in prison about the image of a white Jesus. Through pointed questioning, he gets the teacher to admit that the disciples of Jesus—and Jesus himself—were brown. Afterward, in front of the prisoners working in the shop, he reflects on this long-standing (and ongoing!) deception: "If that don't tell you what a liar the white man is—I don't know what else you need to hear."[39]

If Christianity has whiteness at its heart, then where do nonwhites belong? Baldwin himself wondered, since, in his day, God and Jesus both were white, and he was not. "The blood of the Lamb had not cleansed me in any way whatsoever," Baldwin lamented about his time in the Black church. "I was just as black as I had been the day I was born."[40] Ultimately he could not be part of an American Christianity that elevated white heterosexual men, while women, people of color, Indigenous people, and LGBTQ people were left to fight for scraps and to suffer deprivation and degradation. While Baldwin respected and admired Dr. King and continued to search for the welcome table, church would not be a welcoming place for him for multiple reasons.

Jemar Tisby's *The Color of Compromise* relates the disheartening complicity of Christianity with slavery, racism, and racial violence, a shameful story that encompasses America's entire history—and certainly Baldwin's. Even when enslaved people were granted Christian teaching, as Kelly Brown Douglas suggested, it was a tool for oppression and preservation of the status quo, not for liberation. "To make Christianity compatible with slavery," Tisby writes, white Christians spiritualized equality, since "spiritual freedom did not change one's status as slave or free."[41] Slaves and other nonwhites could thus be rationalized as equal in the eyes of the Lord—if not of the law. Slavery, of course, is not the sole failing of the church, although it is a monumental one. During the Jim Crow era, Christians largely turned a blind eye to lynching, the terrorist attacks that enforced racial hierarchies outside of any legal system. Then through the long and ongoing battle for civil rights, white church leaders consistently trusted the system, even in the face of blatant discrimination and the evidence of horrific living conditions in the inner cities.[42]

Sometimes Christian leaders have simply stood aside in the face of blatant prejudice, which is lamentable enough; I recently heard the Episcopal bishop of Mississippi, Brian Seage, mourn the fact that not a single Mississippi Episcopalian is represented on a wall of heroes in the civil rights museum in Jackson,

Mississippi.[43] Sometimes the religious have stood directly in the way of racial progress; a gathering of seven white Alabama church leaders (and one rabbi) directed the 1963 open letter "A Call for Unity" to Martin Luther King Jr., condemning the demonstrations led by "outside agitators"—and leading to Dr. King's masterful rebuttal and condemnation of the American church titled "Letter from Birmingham Jail."

Even today, the white church remains racist and often unrepentant over its long, hateful, and unchristian history. In recent years, millions of people and many leaders have left the Southern Baptist Convention (SBC) because of the continuing racial and sexual discrimination represented by this powerful religious organization initially formed in support of slavery. In 2020 my friend the Rev. Dr. Ralph West withdrew his Church without Walls, a Houston congregation of some thirty thousand families, from the SBC after a group of seminary presidents attacked the popular bogeyman of Critical Race Theory, proclaiming in effect that the history and ongoing presence of systemic racism would never be taught in Southern Baptist seminaries.

Pastor West was rightly appalled by this decision. "American history has been tainted with racism," he wrote. "America codified it. And more, our public and private institutions propagated it." While the SBC has apologized for its stance on slavery and a Black pastor was brought onstage to accept that apology, as Ralph noted, the Convention's repentance and acknowledgment remained and remain missing from the equation.[44] The most visible Christian movements in America today have become those of white Christian nationalists, preserving the elevated status of white men as Black men continue to die at the hands of a legal system that sees them as a danger.

Black churches face their own challenges. No human institutions are above reproach. In the church of his youth, Baldwin witnessed greed and corruption; he had, he said, "seen too many monstrous things." Most importantly, he wrote, "There was no love in the church. It was a mask for hatred and self-hatred and despair. When we were told to love everybody, I had thought that that meant *everybody*. But no. It applied only to those who believed as we did, and it did not apply to white people at all."[45] Instead of "Faith, Hope, and Charity," Baldwin said that the church seemed to embrace "Blindness, Loneliness, and Terror, the first principle necessarily and actively cultivated in order to deny the two others."[46]

A religious faith that led not to love but to hatred or fear was anathema to Baldwin, who as a young preacher learned it was also anathema to that Jesus who in the Gospel of John called for radical, self-sacrificing love as the greatest value. After washing his disciples' feet—a debasing task meant in that first-century culture to be performed by menials, not by a holy teacher—the Jewish Jesus offers them a beautiful summary of what's most important from all the commandments in the Torah: "Love one another. Just as I have loved you, you also should love one another."[47]

This lies at the heart of what it means to be a community of faith. If a community fails its members in this way, what value can it have for the brokenhearted seeking peace and acceptance? And how can a community that does not love and value each other possibly carry that transforming love outside into a challenging world? In *The Amen Corner*, Sister Margaret is the pious leader of a Holiness church, but her son David discovers that rather than his father Luke abandoning her, the story she had always told him, she abandoned Luke and left him to perish.

Churches can be havens for some within them—and hell for others. Tish, in *If Beale Street Could Talk*, remembers the time she went to the Black Holiness church with her friend—later, lover—Fonny and with his unsufferably holy mother and sisters, and how the voices of the congregation rose but "without any mercy at all." The God of love was not present.[48] And while Baldwin wrote in *One Day When I Was Lost* of a variation on Islam and a different sort of faith community than he knew as a child, Malcolm X was discovering that he had grown to national prominence in a religious movement that had helped to give his life purpose and to teach that God forgives, yet the leaders were willing to sacrifice him to preserve their control of the Nation of Islam's message.

In *The Fire Next Time* and elsewhere, Baldwin was critical of any religious movement whose impelling force was not love. We have mentioned the occasion when his father, David, told him that his Jewish friend was going to hell, a fate with which, Baldwin supposed, he was expected to concur.[49] After having dinner with Elijah Muhammad, leader of the Nation of Islam, Baldwin found himself just as distressed by the movement's exclusion and hatred as he was by any Black Christian or white supremacist movement employing faith as a medium to foment hatred and division. Although faith has a supernatural dimension, religion and religious discourse can be employed in worldly ways. As Baldwin put it, "Heavenly witnesses are a tricky lot, to be used by whoever is closest to Heaven at the time. And legend and theology, which are designed to sanctify our fears, crimes, and aspirations, also reveal them for what they are."[50] For that reason, Baldwin understood the dangerous nature of bad faith: it could be a force for hatred and justify injustice, because in the Western past and in his own experience, it had often done so.

But one of the most startling things about Baldwin is that while he cannot help but write from the standpoint of the marginalized and the persecuted, he recognizes the lostness and agony of the persecutors. Here, indeed is not just one of the most Christian dimensions of Baldwin's faith and hope, but the power of religious belief rightly applied. In his letter to his nephew James, "My Dungeon Shook" in *The Fire Next Time*, I am brought back again and again to Baldwin's invocation of love and compassion as a central part of what he has to teach us:

> There is no reason for you to try to become like white people, and there is no basis whatever for their impertinent assumption that they must accept you. The really terrible thing, old buddy, is that you must accept them. And I mean that very seriously. You must accept them and accept them with love.[51]

American innocence has led to the slaughter of innocents—our own American Holocaust, to be certain, of Indigenous and other peoples—but Baldwin has the presence of mind to see the humanity of those who have oppressed and who still oppress. It's a vital lesson I fear we've lost today despite the so-called Christian character of America. Perhaps it is a special gift of the novelist: like Baldwin, I know that even our most reprehensible characters have reasons for their brokenness. It does not excuse; no one is saying so. But as Faulkner knew, for example, Thomas Sutpen, the frankly horrifying main character of *Absalom, Absalom!* (1936), is as much a product of his life and a victim of that lived experience as he is a victimizer of others. In her play *A Raisin in the Sun* (1959), Baldwin's friend Lorraine Hansberry says that you always have to take into account the hills and valleys a person has traveled.

In *No Name in the Street*, Baldwin wrote about being sexually assaulted by a white southern powerbroker, and as appalling as it was to suffer this unwanted touch, Baldwin was somehow able to muse about the ways in which slavery and Jim Crow had made their white masters inhuman. Baldwin writes of the "abjectness" of the act, the "wet, despairing hands," "the wet, blind eyes," "the despair among the loveless."[52] I have never attained this level of compassion toward those who have damaged me, but then I am not James Baldwin.

This does not of course mean that one papers over the harms—remember Ralph West talking about the ongoing damage caused by the church's failure to repent—but when one begins to think of all human beings as creatures both beloved by God and subject to brokenness, then it becomes possible to find real compassion. All the great villains in my life are also damaged; I can wish that they had responded to their brokenness without harming me or anyone else, yet harm often grows out of harm: hurt people hurt people.

Life is tragic, pain is present, death is inevitable. But where fear and hatred corrode and close us down, love heals and magnifies. This is a central lesson of true faith, and one of Baldwin's most important teachings.

In his 1965 interview with James Mossman, Baldwin said that love was like a fire, like the wind, something that changes you and can change the world.[53] The presiding bishop of the Episcopal Church, the Very Rev. Michael Curry, often says that if God is love, then "If it's not about love, it's not about God."[54] And while Baldwin saw, heard, and experienced much that was not about love, he seems to have understood that this was ultimately where all people of hope and faith must settle. Late in his life he wrote *The Evidence of Things Not Seen*, an extended essay on the murder of Black children in Atlanta—a piece that often found him angry and disgusted with the continuing inequality of Black people in America, with the iniquities of America's justice system, and the slow if not invisible change in our nation. The title is from the Letter to the Hebrews: "Faith is the substance of things hoped for, the evidence of things not seen."[55] Only a few years from the end of his life, after seeing the deaths of many of those he admired and hoped would bring those things hoped for, Baldwin seemed tired and at the end of his rope.

But at the book's end, he recounts encountering a young man from his church on the street, and how this young man, Buddy, had been cast from the community and seemed to him "sad and weary," "lightless and lonely, unbelievably lonely, looking at something far away or deep within."[56] Like Sonny, like Malcolm Little, like Rufus, like Baldwin himself at times, Buddy was lost in every way a human being can be lost. He died not long after, and Baldwin, wrestling with his own feelings about his community, wondered if they might have done something to save him, if love for him might have "made the split-second difference between choosing life and choosing death. All of our lives really hang on some such tiny thread and it is very dangerous not to know this."[57]

Baldwin, you will remember, had been taught early in his life in the church that we are called to love everybody. "Whoever else did not believe this," he remembers, "*I* did." And thus, to talk about a faith community—about any community—one has to acknowledge the primacy of love, "our endless connection with, and responsibility for, each other."[58]

To the end of his life, Baldwin spoke of the concept of the welcome table, a place where this brotherhood and sisterhood, this kind of love, this kind of unity might be possible. The concept comes from a spiritual that was also sung in the civil rights era. Its first verse proclaims, "I'm going to sit at the Welcome Table one of these days." Perhaps just now, I am alone, hungry, sad, lost. But someday, somewhere, there will be a place where I belong. Where I will be seen and known. Where I will be accepted. Where I will be welcome at the feast alongside all my brothers and sisters. One of these days, I'm going to sit at the Welcome Table.

This was an article of faith for Baldwin. If we did not succumb to fear and hatred, if we did not implode from our own divisions, such a thing was attainable. In *The Welcome Table*, Baldwin writes about the diverse communities he had witnessed at the dinner table of his friend the actress and activist Josephine Baker—and at his own home, both of them in the South of France. The cast of *The Welcome Table* is white and Black and Arab, Christian and Muslim and unbeliever, gay and straight, married and divorced, old and young, exiles and travelers and homebodies. Regina, an old friend of the famous expatriate actress Edith, whose house in the South of France is the setting of the play—tells Edith she has gathered a spectacularly diverse cast of characters—all of them with their own pain and loss and regret, but all of them with the possibility of change and growth, particularly in a loving community gathered together and willing to tell each other healing truths. Peter, the journalist who has come to the South of France to interview Edith, says at the end of the play that he feels himself breaking up like ice on the river in the direct sunshine, that (in less poetic terms) he is being broken down and reformed and will become something more, something better as a result of this community that has engaged him.

It is a play full of religious language and reference. Peter calls on the Lord for help and confesses that he loves his son more than he believes in the hope of his own salvation. Two characters discuss Jesus's parable of the Good Samaritan, a story about a hated and reviled member of a marginalized group who rescues a Jew who falls among thieves, one of Jesus's most important teachings about our responsibility to others. But most important is the concept of the Welcome Table at the heart of the play and referenced directly at its very end. It represents what Baldwin believed—that love is powerful, true community is possible, and one of these days all of us may sit together.

At the end of his life, for all his denials, Baldwin still had faith in something very much like the church he longed to see and perhaps to be part of: a place of refuge, welcome, encouragement, and transformation driven by love, respect, and shared responsibility. It's a shame that no one has ever seen this play, but please take my word that it is a powerful and grace-filled work that aptly sums up the beliefs, hopes, and longings of its author.

And of many of us, also searching for such a place.

Baldwin on Race

Blacks have never been free in this
country, never was it intended that
they be free.... A civilized country is,
by definition, a country dominated by whites,
in which the blacks clearly know their place.

—James Baldwin, *No Name in the Streets*

Over the years, I've introduced many people to James Bald-win—and to the problem of race and justice in America—by screening or teaching the documentary film *I Am Not Your Negro* (2016). In Raoul Peck's Academy Award–nominated film, we watch a range of Baldwin's many public appearances—a 1969 interview on the *Dick Cavett Show,* a segment from his famous 1965 debate at Cambridge with William F. Buckley, and the film's painful titular line from a 1963 conversation with the noted Black intellectual Kenneth B. Clark—and discover that they all revolve around race and Baldwin's thoughts about American life.[1]

For all his fame, Baldwin's essays, speeches, and advocacy for equity and civil rights placed him in a remarkable position over his final decades. He was frequently called upon to explain to white people what was happening in Black culture: the voting drives and marches; arguments about violence versus nonviolence within Black culture; towering figures such as Dr. Martin Luther King Jr., Malcolm X, and Medgar Evers; and the simple fact that while the minds of some whites might be changing, they were certainly not doing so fast enough—or markedly enough—to address America's "race problem."

In his appearance with Dick Cavett, Baldwin waves off a question about whether "the Negroes" are optimistic about the future. The question, Baldwin says, is not simply about Black people and their current mood or circumstances. "The real question," he argues, here and throughout his career, "is what is going to happen to this country." Race, the treatment and attitudes of people of color, and this nation's past, present, and future are, Baldwin said, interlinked. The issue of racism and the experiment we call America cannot be understood apart from each other, and America itself will rise or fall based on how it ultimately deals—or does not deal—with those interrelated issues.

So it is that Baldwin guides us into conversation about race and racism—what it is, how it works, why it exists—as he also directs us into conversation about the America where racism has been endemic throughout history. What he was saying was that the story of Black people in America was, in a very real sense, the story of the nation, and until we were willing to acknowledge that truth, excavate that history, and repent the very great sins of that past, present, and future, we could not hope to make any sort of progress toward the soaring words of the founders, no matter that, as Cavett points out, "There are Negro mayors.

There are Negroes in all of sports. There are Negroes in politics. They are even accorded the ultimate accolade of being in television commercials."[2]

It's important to acknowledge that Baldwin did not think of race—or of the resulting prejudice of racism—as a natural phenomenon. He understood that race is, instead, a construct, a mythic structure erected by white men, especially, in order to subjugate Black people (and others who were not white men), a story that many white people had lived in for so long that they couldn't see the dimensions unless the architecture was pointed out to them. Baldwin said that whiteness was created as a mirror image of Blackness, as a way of elevating some and enslaving others, yet the ultimate result was so demeaning and enslaving to all who were caught up in this worldview—which is to say, all of us—and there was no hope until we threw off the chains of racial thinking.

Baldwin saw racism as damaging to all who are caught up in its lies. It was, though, Black people, Indigenous people, and other people of color who were most powerfully affected by the construction and application of race, by the overwhelming weight of racism in the United States and elsewhere. This was Baldwin's own lived experience, the reality of reckoning with racism on a daily basis in the nation of his birth. "I know what Black Americans endure," he wrote in *No Name in the Street*, "know it in my own flesh and spirit, know it by the human wreckage through which I have passed."[3]

He'd grown up in Harlem, which was in many respects a prison camp for Black people. On more than one occasion, he traveled in the South and encountered official and unofficial systems of repression and violence intended to keep Black people in their places long after legal slavery had gone. During a visit to California, where he went to work on his screenplay about Malcolm X, he drove out to Watts and was reminded, as ever, about the unfavorable conditions under which people who looked like him labored simply because of their skin color:

> How spare, shabby, and dark the houses are. One sees that garbage collection is scarcely more efficient here than it is in Harlem ... the shabby pool halls, the plethora of churches and lodges and liquor stores, the shining automobiles, the wine bottles in the gutter, the garbage-strewn alleys, and the young people, boys and girls in the streets. Over it all hangs a miasma of fury and frustration, a perceptible darkening, as of storm clouds, of rage and despair.[4]

When he spoke and wrote and marched against racism, he was doing so having himself been victimized by it, having seen those he loved minimized and brutalized and sometimes murdered because of their race; and the simple fact that Baldwin was able to get to the end of his life without being caught up in hate for people who look like me—that he was able to love us and understand that we too are caught up in that web of lies sold to us as freedom—makes his lessons on race and America that much more powerful.

He was clear about the fact that race is not a natural or scientific set of human divisions, and that racism is not a normal or healthy human response to perceived physical differences. Few people short of slaveholders, eugenicists, and Nazis have ever professed to believe so. In this understanding that race is an imaginative construct with a defined set of repressive goals, Baldwin fits squarely into the mainstream of thinking.

Historian Barbara Fields, in her groundbreaking essay "Ideology and Race in American History," pushed back against any unthinking understanding that race is real, "a thing, rather than a notion that is profoundly and in its very essence ideological."[5] Similarly, theologian Reggie Williams explained in a 2022 lecture how "the creation of 'Black' is meant to inform the ascendency of white," and that racism and white supremacy are the same thing.[6] Kelly Brown Douglas agrees: "Whiteness is not a biological or an ethnic given. Rather, it is a socially constructed demarcation of race that serves as a badge of privilege and power. It fuels white supremacy, which in turn exists to protect it."[7]

"Race" is a created set of distinctions, and for that matter, as historians like Ibram Kendi acknowledge, recent distinctions, no more than a few hundred years old.[8] The ancient Greeks did not think of themselves and others in terms of race; like many peoples, they broke "them" and "us" down in terms of tribal or national origin. "Barbarians" were people who were not Greeks. British historian David Olusoga notes that we know about the earliest Black people to visit Britain, Roman soldiers, not because they were described by their skin color, but by the identification of their homes in Africa.[9]

It's not until Europeans—which must, of course, include American colonists—began to hold enslaved Africans and to wrestle with the legal and moral implications of that action that race started to enter the picture as a way of differentiating one group from another for the benefit of the group holding power. "The doctrine of white supremacy, which still controls most white people, is itself a stupendous delusion," Baldwin said, "but to be born in America is an immediate, a mortal challenge."[10]

It's clear from early in his career that these ideas about race and racism—that they are artificially constructed concepts intended to keep white people ascendant and Black people in subjugation—inform Baldwin's thinking. In "My Dungeon Shook," the letter to his nephew James that opens *The Fire Next Time*, Baldwin speaks about how his father, David's grandfather, "was defeated long before he died because, at the bottom of his heart, he really believed what white people said about him.... You can only be destroyed by believing that you really are what the white world calls a *nigger*. I tell you this because I love you, and please don't you ever forget it."[11]

That particular myth or set of delusions (as Baldwin called it in *No Name in the Street*) can make white people see Black people as monsters—or make Black people see themselves as such.[12] In an interview with the *Paris Review*, Baldwin said that "insofar as the American public creates a monster, they are not about to recognize it. You create a monster and destroy it. It is part of the American way of life."[13] He talked about how he'd grown up watching John Wayne kill Indians or Tarzan kill Africans, and realized that he had bought into a myth of white supremacy so pervasive that even a small Black boy from Harlem was cheering a white hero destroying people who looked like himself.

In a 1961 interview with journalist Studs Terkel, Baldwin spoke at length about how Black people are "menaced" by a culture that elevates whiteness as the ultimate standard of value:

> Everyone, every Negro in America is, you know, in some way, one way or another, menaced by it. One's born in a white country, in a white, Protestant, Puritan country, where one was once a slave, and where all the standards and all the images that you open your, when you open your eyes in the world, everything you see, none of it applies to you. You go to white movies and, you know, and like everybody else you fall in love with Joan Crawford, or, and you root for the good guys who are killing

off the Indians, and it comes as a great psychological collision when you begin to realize that all of these things are
really metaphors for your oppression and will lead into a
kind of psychological warfare in which you may perish.

Not only are Black people conditioned to compare themselves
to these ultimate white standards of value—until very recently,
white images and even a white God were always presented as
normative—their own reality is ignored within a racist society.
White people don't actually see people of color, Baldwin argued,
not as themselves: "What [white people] do see when they look
at you is what they have invested you with."[14] "You" are the sav-
age, the subhuman, the unintelligent, the unserious—whatever
it is that white people need to see when they regard people of
color and use that vision to define themselves in opposition to it.

So it is that in his 1963 appearance on television with Martin Luther King Jr., Malcolm X, and Kenneth B. Clark, the
climactic moment in the film *I Am Not Your Negro*, Baldwin
said of these racist myths, "What white people have to do is try
to find out in their own hearts why it was necessary to have a
'nigger' in the first place. Because I'm not a nigger, I'm a man.
But if you think I'm a nigger, it means you need him."[15] In a
later interview with Kalamu ya Salaam, Baldwin argued that
"white people invented black people to protect themselves
against something which frightened them."[16] That invention,
we know, was about power and privilege, about the fear of losing those things, and it is an invention that continues to shape
the lives of individuals and of nations.

What gives these racist myths their power is that they are
multifaceted lines of attack ranging across all the ways that
human beings think, speak, and define. Americans cling to their
harmful dreams, Baldwin wrote, because they are "very carefully

and deliberately conditioned" to believe them by news, religion, literature, popular culture, advertising, science, economics, politics; every form of discourse expressing every white racist myth has been used to create an artificial sense of distinctives that were all too real in the way they have played out in the Black lives that were shaped by them, including those of Baldwin, his father, his friends, and his family.[17]

He wrote about these myths in detail, wrestling with them in essays and in narrative form in his fiction and drama. The white church was one of those American mythmakers used to justify racial hierarchy. One reason Baldwin stepped away from the church was that he felt Christianity had failed Black people, that the God presented to him and others was a white God, and that no amount of prayer or time on his knees or faithful service would make him resemble that God the slightest bit more. As we saw, American religion has failed and does fail in ways that Baldwin noted to make the lives of Black people (and indeed of many people) better, more just, more equitable.

"Negroes in this country," he wrote in *The Fire Next Time*, "are taught really to despise themselves from the moment their eyes open on the world. The world is white and they are black. White people hold the power, which means they are superior to blacks (intrinsically, that is: God decreed it so), and the world has innumerable ways of making this difference known and felt and feared."[18] For all the powerful countermyths about race and justice properly advanced by Christians during the civil rights era (Baldwin told Kenneth B. Clark that Dr. King was "a very rare, a very great man. Martin's rare for two reasons: probably just because he is, and because he's a real Christian"), the American church has been responsible for too many justifications of slavery and segregation, from lying sermons preached from illustrious pulpits to that patronizing open letter in 1963 from southern clergy to Dr. King that prompted his "Letter from Birmingham Jail."[19]

American culture was and is another powerful mythmaker. In *Go Tell It on the Mountain*, young John Grimes goes to a movie on his fourteenth birthday—an action forbidden by the strict Pentecostal practice of his family. The film seems to have been 1934's *Of Human Bondage* starring Bette Davis and Leslie Howard. Although John decides to see the movie because he identifies with the defeated-seeming "blonde young man" on the movie poster (Howard), once he's in the midst of it, he finds himself being seduced by the "blonde, and pasty white" woman who treats the young student with such callousness and contempt.[20] Although Helen Brown Norden, a contemporary reviewer from *Vanity Fair*, calls Miss Davis's role "one of the most thoroughly unsympathetic characters the screen has ever produced: vicious, cheap, shallow, despicable," John finds himself identifying with her more and more as the movie immerses him in the story: "He wanted to be like her, only more powerful, more thorough, and more cruel."[21] The mythmaking power of the silver screen could—and still does—reinforce myths and immerse us in stories, and films can galvanize audiences to thoughtful action, or put them back to sleep.

In that powerful debate performance against conservative intellectual William F. Buckley over the question "Has the American Dream been achieved at the expense of the American Negro?" Baldwin pointed out that whiteness is depicted as the only desirable identity in our culture, and returns to his refrain that the movies of his youth—and past—were products or perhaps even tools of American racism: "It comes as a great shock around the age of five, or six, or seven, to discover that Gary Cooper killing off the Indians when you were rooting for Gary Cooper, that the Indians were you. It comes as a great shock to discover the country which is your birthplace and to which you owe your life and your identity has not in its whole system of reality evolved any place for you."[22]

Baldwin was a thoughtful consumer of movies and drama from his childhood, when his teacher Bill Miller took him to screenings and performances. In the book-length critical essay *The Devil Finds Work*, Baldwin reflects on the ways Hollywood concocted a cocktail of escapism and racism. He argues that movie stars offer "escape personalities," none of whom (at least before Sidney Poitier came along) is ever Black. "That the movie star is an 'escape' personality," he argues, "indicates one of the irreducible dangers to which the moviegoer is exposed: the danger of surrendering to the corroboration of one's fantasies as they are thrown back from the screen."[23]

Another irreducible danger is seen in the way Hollywood traditionally approached race—by reinforcing the attitudes of a racist society. Baldwin describes *The Birth of a Nation* (1915) in *The Devil Finds Work* as a cinematic masterwork, "one of the great classics of the American cinema," which is also "an elaborate justification of mass murder."[24] In less overtly racist films—and even some attempting to display a countercultural tolerance and awareness of racism—Baldwin nonetheless calls out where they fall short—and why they must, given their primarily white audience.[25] His comments on *The Defiant Ones* (1958), *In the Heat of the Night* (1967), and *Guess Who's Coming to Dinner* (1967)—all featuring Sidney Poitier—reveal attempts to sugarcoat or circumvent racism through their stories.[26]

Elsewhere in *The Devil Finds Work*, Baldwin noted how *Guess Who's Coming to Dinner*'s use of a familiar Mammy character for comic relief militates against whatever liberal impulses the movie possesses. Baldwin noted in his criticism that films for white audiences often reinforced stereotypes and racist tropes; those audiences seemed to need the lies of the culture confirmed, not called out.

I've written on how American film and television have been part of a slowly shifting national movement from racism to anti-racism, but there's no question that for decades these two hugely influential cultural forms misrepresented—or completely omitted—people of color. In some of the most important films in history—*Birth of a Nation* being one, *Gone with the Wind* another—racist ideologies were front and center, part of the primary appeal of the film to white audiences. In her 2022 book, *The Wrath to Come: Gone with the Wind and the Lies America Tells*, historian Sarah Churchwell takes on the Lost Cause myth powerfully. She told me, "It's partly that [the movie] shapes our thinking and partly that it captures our thinking—it registers America's myths about itself and the desires that drive those myths, the desire to maintain our own sense of innocence at all costs, which is perhaps the most fundamental desire."[27]

In his understanding of these myths and inventions, Baldwin would agree with Churchwell's formulation: that what white America wants more than anything is to maintain its sense of innocence, and also its ignorance, since they are directly linked.

People need to believe in their innocence and will do much to preserve it. Historian Tyler Stovall notes in *White Freedom: The Racial History of an Idea* that people don't consciously choose evil; they choose a myth or myths they can hide behind, that can allow them to avert their eyes from such a judgment. Stovall notes, "The construction of white freedom rested on the idea that both liberty and white racial identity were not only positive values but also in many ways inseparable."[28] Innocence and ignorance were and are essential tools in the maintenance of white sanity—and simultaneously of white supremacy.

Baldwin understood this, and how innocence and ignorance were reasons for the behavior of so many white Americans, rather than excuses for it. When he encouraged his nephew to have love for the oppressor, as we read earlier, it was out of his understanding of how many white Americans are caught in their myths: "The danger," he told his nephew, "in the minds of most white Americans is the loss of their identity." It is a terrifying thing, he said, to discover that the world is not what you imagined it to be.[29] Easier, perhaps, to hide behind innocence, ignorance, or even denial.

In the introduction to his play *Blues for Mister Charlie*, Baldwin wrote that "no man is a villain in his own eyes. Something in the man knows—must know—that what he is doing is evil; but in order to accept the knowledge, the man would have to change." The only other choice—because many people do not choose awareness and change—is to "close his eyes," continue in his crimes, and slide into spiritual darkness.[30]

White Americans, he argued, were thus at the same time the most innocent—and the most dangerous—people on earth. Our celebrated founding myths circled around violence and subjugation: "The real meaning and history of Manifest Destiny, for example, is nothing less than calculated and deliberate genocide. But American folklore, which has seduced American history into a radiant stupor, transforms the slaughter into a heroic legend. Since the legend has obliterated the truth," he says in *The Evidence of Things Not Seen*, it is all but impossible for white people to comprehend the realities of Indigenous people or people of color.[31] This clutched-for innocence is understandable, because the problems of race, hatred, and discrimination are so deeply damaging and so seemingly insoluble, but that does not mean they should be hidden behind a veil of innocence.

In "My Dungeon Shook," the opening letter of *The Fire Next Time*, Baldwin uses the word "innocence" or some variant a number of times in the opening pages: "these innocent and well-meaning people"; "I hear the chorus of the innocents screaming, 'No! This is not true! How bitter you are!'"; "This innocent country set you down in a ghetto in which, in fact, it intended that you should perish."[32] You do not have to be a professor of literature to know that authors employ repetition to call attention to something, to assign it a larger dimension, to give it a twist, so it should not be surprising that Baldwin complicates the concept by repetition and through one of his great aphorisms: "It is not permissible that the authors of devastation should also be innocent. It is the innocence that constitutes the crime."[33]

He equated innocence with ignorance. In *Another Country*, he creates several white liberals who seem to want to get past the "race question," and who to Baldwin seem to be like Hollywood liberals, wanting to do the right thing but not knowing what the right thing truly is. (They lack commitment, which, as Baldwin said, is simple: "You mean it or you don't."[34]) Rufus, who is Black, thinks sadly about his friend Vivaldo that Vivaldo didn't understand his white countrymen.[35] Through the rest of the novel, Vivaldo often demonstrates this ignorance: how for all his good intentions, he doesn't understand the effects of racism on people of color, and how maybe, just maybe, he is refusing to tell the hard truth about race, although at least he does at one point imagine that perhaps some part of Rufus hated and feared him because he, Vivaldo, was white, and perhaps some part of Vivaldo had hated and feared Rufus because he was Black.[36]

Vivaldo's ignorance and innocence play out frequently in Vivaldo's interracial relationship with Rufus's sister Ida. Many of their conversations and conflicts revolve around race, and particularly around Vivaldo's failure to understand his words or actions from Ida's perspective. Another well-meaning white liberal, Cass, tries to understand the Black viewpoints of Rufus and later, Ida, but like Vivaldo, still seems unable to appreciate the scope of the problem. White people—like herself—are well meaning. Isn't the world getting better for Black people? A part of her remains startled and surprised by the depth of harmful racial feeling on both sides.

Baldwin knew something about white liberals who thought they were racially progressive. Think of Dick Cavett's somewhat-condescending (and perhaps ironic) statement/question to Baldwin about the rapidly improving lot of the Negro. Baldwin—like other people of color I know who write, speak, preach, or profess about race and justice—surely had to deal with his share of well-meaning whites who say they are in sympathy, that they want things to change, but who remain unaware of so much. One of the most startling examples of this in Baldwin's life and in American history was the tense racial summit with Attorney General Robert F. Kennedy in May 1963. Kennedy, who was in favor of measured racial progress, asked Baldwin to gather a group of Black artists and advocates to meet with him and Department of Justice lawyer Burke Marshall in the Kennedy penthouse in Manhattan.[37] Baldwin invited a number of people involved in the fight for racial freedom, including Harry Belafonte, Lorraine Hansberry, Lena Horne, white actor Rip Torn, Kenneth Clark, and Baldwin's brother David.

Kennedy had asked that Martin Luther King Jr. and leaders of the NAACP not be present, because he hoped to gauge how Baldwin and his guests felt about their leadership. Kennedy also wanted to lay out the racial accomplishments of his administration, to explain the political realities of why change moved so slowly, and to try to get some understanding of the rage and despair among Black people when—as he felt—things were changing for the better. Why were people being drawn to Black Power and to Malcolm X instead of to peaceful protest? Why didn't they trust their government to bring about incremental change?

The attorney general seems to have imagined this meeting in his family's apartment off Central Park as a familiar and comfortable situation: a powerful white man explaining how things were, a Black audience nodding their heads and perhaps offering some words of thanks or confirmation or encouragement.

But that is precisely what did not happen, thanks to Jerome Smith, who was just twenty-four years old, a former Freedom Rider and an organizer who had suffered horrific personal violence in the Deep South, and was in New York at that time to receive medical care for the latest attack he'd endured. After listening to Kennedy extol the accomplishments of the administration and lament the political problem of how racist southern Democrats were reacting to Black rage, Smith told him that he didn't know why he was here listening to "all this cocktail-party patter."

Smith explained to Kennedy that it wasn't Black Muslims who were the threat; it was people like himself, Black advocates of peaceful protest and organizing who were losing their hope. He told Kennedy that he was at the edge of his strength and the edge of his patience and could not promise to keep turning the other cheek if the police kept coming at him with dogs, billy clubs, and firehoses. "When I pull a trigger," he said, "kiss it goodbye." Then he shocked the attorney general further by telling him that young Black people who were forced to fight for their rights at home would not fight for this country in Vietnam or anywhere else.

Kennedy turned away from Smith, startled and angry, and scanned the room. Was there a more civilized voice, one who could listen to reason, who understood the political realities better than this boy? Surely some of these others could speak a word of moderation. But playwright Lorraine Hansberry turned the attention back to Jerome Smith: "You've got a great many very, very accomplished people in this room, Mr. Attorney General, but the only man who should be listened to is that man over there."

Kennedy felt ambushed. This sort of direct confrontation was uncivil and perhaps, he thought, ungrateful. I suspect that like many well-intentioned whites, Kennedy was powerfully shaped by American myths of freedom, justice, and well-meaning power, and he could not understand why these leaders—including this young man—were so angry, so unyielding, so unwilling to listen, so unwilling to love and trust their country. Kennedy's own temper rose, and the evening ended badly. Hansberry coolly told him good night and walked out, and the others followed.

Historian Larry Tye writes, "Neither side got what it wanted. The blacks had grasped the chance to vent their rage—one reason they'd come on such short notice. They had also hoped to remake this well-meaning brother of a president into an ally, not for his incremental reforms but for breakthrough change. The blacks believed they had not only failed but that they had burned the bridge they had come to build."[38] James Baldwin and Kenneth Clark went directly from the meeting to a TV studio, arriving late for that program on which they would discuss the racial divide with Dr. King and Malcolm X. Baldwin remained visibly angry and upset about the events of the evening, which can be observed in his on-air responses.

Robert F. Kennedy had come into this meeting with Baldwin and his cohorts as a well-meaning white man who assumed he knew what was best and that his country was on an upward trajectory in regard to race. He represented good white liberals. What he found instead was the truth: Black people were weary and angry and in despair because most of the people in this nation live in denial of the horrible facts of racism. Even many good white liberals.

This meeting might be an emotional scene worthy of a James Baldwin novel, complicated and interesting characters talking past—or shouting at—each other because they come from different backgrounds. A scene where white characters maintain that they are not themselves racist. Or that they don't see color. A scene where no connections are made, no growth occurs, no change happens.

But thankfully, that is not what transpired. Yes, Kennedy was incensed and outraged in the moment and for some little time after. He was puzzled as to how a room full of American citizens, even Black ones, could have such radically different conceptions about American issues, and he ordered phones tapped and greater surveillance on Baldwin and other attendees—presumably because he now saw them as a greater danger to peace and security. (I do not like this fact, because I admire RFK, but facts matter. He did this, and Baldwin later confronted FBI agents who wanted to search his apartment.)

But to his credit—and thankfully for American history—something shifted in Bobby Kennedy. In Christian teaching, we often refer to the New Testament Greek word *metanoia*, which is typically translated as "repentance." In the church of my youth, that was the big idea: stop doing those bad things you shouldn't be doing. But the actual translation from the Greek is more nuanced: it's not simply about stopping what you shouldn't do, but about a 180-degree turn toward what you should do. Stop doing these bad things, and lean into these good things. As Baldwin put it, we can always be and do better.

Mark Whitaker noted in the *Washington Post* that Bobby "matured for the better over time, from his days as an aide to red-baiter Joe McCarthy and attack-dog attorney general for JFK. Bobby Kennedy was one of the rare leaders in our national history who appeared to grow wiser, humbler, and more compassionate the more fame and power he attained."[39] Only a few weeks after he was schooled at Baldwin's civil rights meeting, Kennedy became the lone presidential adviser encouraging JFK to respond to the segregationist actions of Governor George Wallace in Alabama by giving a substantial speech on civil rights.

In fact, RFK and Burke Marshall worked with speechwriter Ted Sorensen on the speech the president delivered on national television on June 11, 1963, a speech that leaned into all the things that the assembled civil rights leaders had wanted Bobby Kennedy to understand in May. Bobby also sat with his brother in the twenty minutes before he went on air, helping him script additional talking points. As Eric Michael Dyson notes, Baldwin and the others had wanted Kennedy to understand, "This was not just about politics; it was about morality, dignity, about taking a symbolic stand in front of the entire country. [Robert] Kennedy didn't get that. He kept insisting that change was hard and slow."[40] But the speech RFK helped his brother deliver that night shows that those lessons were not wasted, that a serious confrontation had also led to some hard reassessments.

In that nationally broadcast speech, President Kennedy went further than any previous American president in calling out racism as a national sin:

We are confronted primarily with a moral issue. It is
as old as the scriptures and is as clear as the American
Constitution.... The heart of the question is whether
all Americans are to be afforded equal rights and equal
opportunities, whether we are going to treat our fellow
Americans as we want to be treated. If an American,
because his skin is dark, cannot eat lunch in a restaurant
open to the public, if he cannot send his children to the
best public school available, if he cannot vote for the public officials who will represent him, if, in short, he cannot
enjoy the full and free life which all of us want, then who
among us would be content to have the color of his skin
changed and stand in his place? Who among us would
then be content with the counsels of patience and delay?[41]

By describing racism as a "moral crisis," the president said
that even though there must be constructive political actions,
this was, at heart, an issue about what sort of nation America
would be, an issue to be decided in every American heart—
language very much like Baldwin's own in saying that the race
question would determine whether the American experiment
would succeed or fail. This moral crisis, Kennedy said, called
for all Americans to do the tough work of democracy, since the
problem could not "be quieted by token moves or talk. It is
time to act in the Congress, in your State and local legislative
body and, above all, in all of our daily lives. It is not enough to
pin the blame on others, to say this is a problem of one section
of the country or another, or deplore the fact that we face [it]. A
great change is at hand, and our task, our obligation, is to make
that revolution, that change, peaceful and constructive for all."[42]

John F. Kennedy proposed landmark civil rights legislation,
which Lyndon Johnson saw through Congress after Kennedy's

assassination. Bobby Kennedy, in the years following his painful racial cocktail party, developed a love and understanding for the poor, for the downtrodden of every race, and for those held down by white supremacy. As a senator and as a candidate for president, RFK showed how the witness Baldwin often spoke of could bear fruit.

Yet John Kennedy's speech calling for race to be treated as a national issue of what is right and moral was almost sixty years ago at the time of this writing, just as Bobby Kennedy has now been dead for over fifty years, and racist movements are back in the headlines, particularly white Christian nationalism, which was implicated in the January 6, 2021, assault on the Capitol and the 2022 massacre of Black shoppers in Buffalo, New York. The quiet part is now being said out loud in the "replacement theory" myth espoused by politicians and television commentators. Scholars Samuel L. Perry and Philip S. Gorski are among many observers who say that white Christian nationalism represents the most dangerous threat to American democracy, while in a trip through the looking glass, white evangelical Protestants are, according to a 2021 poll from PRRI, revealed as "the religious group most likely to agree that true American patriots might have to resort to violence in order to save our country."[43]

We seem to have slid backward or sideways since Baldwin's time. The great irony of these statements is that living in the dream, with our eyes closed, or listening more to the formative myths than to reality, damages everybody touched by those myths—Black children in Harlem or Watts, Black men tortured and lynched in the Deep South, motorists put at risk for driving while Black, and Black families prevented from moving into a better neighborhood or exposed to environmental dangers.

But also white families in suburbia. White soccer moms. White-collar white executives. Bubbas in Texas. Confederate flag wavers in Alabama. White Christian nationalists all over America.

To be a human treated as an animal is devastating, Baldwin said, and he offered plenty of dramatic and real-life explanations of the great harms visited on Black people by white supremacy. Note—just as one example—his summary of grievances in the Cambridge Union debate with William F. Buckley: "Leaving aside all the physical facts that one can quote. Leaving aside rape or murder. Leaving aside the bloody catalog of oppression, which we are in one way too familiar with already, what this does to the subjugated, the most private, the most serious thing this does to the subjugated, is to destroy his sense of reality."[44]

 All of that is bad enough, and certainly no right-thinking person could argue with the fact that Indigenous people and people of color have suffered much at the hands of white Americans. But to be a human treating another human as an animal is horrible in its own way. In a 1967 interview with Cep Dergisi, Baldwin said that myths about Black inferiority had initially been laid out to provide moral justification for slavery: "If you buy and sell a man like an animal, then you must persuade yourself that he is an animal." The moral calculus, Baldwin says, is, "The man who is being used like an animal exerts all his energy in not becoming one; while the man who is so using him fatally descends in the human scale and becomes something much worse than an animal."[45]

Baldwin was clear that the moral damage done to white people by racism was soul-killing, that white people experienced daily damage from oppressing just as—in a more direct way—Black people took daily damage from being oppressed. He said so to his nephew, in explaining why he must love white people. He said so in his Malcolm X screenplay, when he recorded Malcolm's post-hajj recognition that white people were not inherently evil, were not the white devils of Black Muslim thought, but were caught in a kind of prison made by the twin evils of Christianity and capitalism.[46]

My friend Robert P. Jones took the title for his book *White Too Long: The Legacy of White Supremacy in American Christianity* from Baldwin's 1969 article in the *New York Times* where he remarked, "I will flatly say that the bulk of this country's white population impresses me, and has so impressed me for a very long time, as being beyond any conceivable hope of moral rehabilitation. They have been white, if I may so put it, too long."[47] By this, Baldwin—and Robby Jones—were exploring the dimensions of the deep hole white people have dug for themselves. In his review of *White Too Long*, Jemar Tisby asked a question familiar to Frederick Douglass and to Baldwin: If *White Too Long* "convincingly reveals the myriad ways that white Christianity has cultivated the religious, political, economic and social superiority of white people," is there anything left to save?[48] In connection with integration, Baldwin sometimes used the metaphor of being invited to move into a burning house. Who would want to do that?

Theologian Reggie Williams has remarked, "You can either confront racism or accept it," and my years of reading Baldwin and working against racism bear this out.[49] Too many Americans accept it—or lean into it—and the problem continues, festers. The frustration that Baldwin's guests expressed to Robert Kennedy was about treating racism with political gradualism instead of seeing it as an existential moral issue.

Black people die at the hands of police, or from environmental exposure, or from inadequate care.

White people rot from the moral decay of white supremacy.

So the pressing questions for which we should be seeking

Baldwin's guidance here have to be: How can we confront racism in America? How can we be *committed* to that fight?

It's a question that people have considered for four hundred years. Living separately, living apart, doing real or symbolic violence to each other, hating each other, looking past each other—all of these have been talked about and tried. Slavery, formal and informal segregation, sending Black people back to Africa (or driving white devils into the sea), murdering each other in our beds, refusing to acknowledge color—all of these are historical examples of avoidance with differing degrees of hostility attached. But what may be most disheartening to many of us, I'm convinced that Baldwin would not be surprised by the need for a Black Lives Matter movement, but he would shake his head sadly at how America has backslid on overt racism after—and perhaps in reaction to—electing its first Black president. In an Emmy-winning comedy special, John Mulaney captured the shock many of us felt after the 2017 white supremacist march in Charlottesville, the perhaps foolish thought that America was on an upward moral trajectory on race: "And now there are Nazis again!? ... I don't care for these new Nazis, and you can quote me on that."[50] It's a funny bit—just as it's appalling that we should have to face these old evils in their new guises.

As we noted, white supremacists in the public eye and even in public office continue to mutter their vile racist lies and roll out the old racist myths, and it has its intended effect: to hurt, quiet, and kill Black people. "Let us tell it like it is," Baldwin wrote, listing a roll call of racists of his day, and saying that their rhetoric, "historically and actually, has brought death to untold numbers of people, and it was meant to bring death to them."[51] Black people could respond to verbal and physical attacks in kind—Malcolm X's famous "by any means necessary" defense—but Baldwin believed that returning hatred for hatred was a loser's game.

Imagining that we can live separately—on this continent or on any other—is also a ridiculous notion. We cannot separate from each other, despite the desires of white supremacists, the Nation of Islam, and even many abolitionists (Abraham Lincoln was originally in favor of repatriating Black people to Africa). In the essay "Stranger in the Village," where he contemplated his time spent in Switzerland, Baldwin reached some conclusions that shaped his understandings about race forever: "I am a stranger here. But I am not a stranger in America."[52] In America, we are stuck with each other. We cannot hide behind the innocence excuse. Baldwin notes, "American white men still nourish the illusion that there is some means of recovering the European innocence, of returning to a state in which black men do not exist. This is one of the greatest errors Americans can make. . . . People who shut their eyes to reality simply invite their own destruction, and anyone who insists on remaining in a state of innocence long after this innocence is dead turns himself into a monster."[53]

Forget about the experience of those white men, women, and children in Switzerland who had regarded Baldwin as an exotic circus act, a one-off phenomenon. Black people and white people in America were members of the same family—sometimes literally—and could not turn their backs on each other. I am not going to vanish, Baldwin said, and neither is the Black Muslim goal of conquest possible: "I can't drive all white people into the seas and you can't send me back to Africa. We're going to have to make this revolution here—together—or not at all."[54] In another interview, he reiterated this truth: "I'm related to the white American by blood; I don't have an English name for nothing. . . . We cannot separate. The tragedy of the white people is that they always thought they could."[55]

Nothing will change. Until something changes. "The price of the liberation of the white people is the liberation of the blacks," Baldwin wrote toward the end of *The Fire Next Time*, "the total liberation, in the cities, in the towns, before the law, and in the mind.... We, the black and the white, deeply need each other here if we are really to become a nation—if we are really, that is, to achieve our identity, our maturity, as men and women."[56] We need each other.

What I've been learning about confronting racism in the course of wrestling with it in classrooms, churches, and elsewhere is that there are a set of steps, spelled out for us by Baldwin and others, that might lead to a better future. My own formulation of it for people who look like me is alliterative: recognition, relationship, and repair, with repentance thrown in as a recurring circular act. Not surprisingly, given his influence on me, this seems to be the way Baldwin understands the work of racial healing. We must confront our past honestly—history is very important to Baldwin—telling the truth about it, and recognizing that what is at the heart of racism is not political or economic or religious or anything but moral. Racism is an undiluted wrong. Black and white both must address history. That white people must grapple with history and tell the truth about it is obvious, but Baldwin's vision was more expansive. We all had to tell the truth: "To accept one's past—one's history—is not the same thing as drowning in it; it is learning how to use it. An invented past can never be used; it cracks and crumbles under the pressure of life like clay in a season of drought."[57]

The word Baldwin constantly uses is "witness," so let's open that up. To be a witness is to tell the truth about the lives we're living, the lies we're living. It is to stand up and say what is wrong—and what is right. Think of all those Baldwin speeches, TV appearances, interviews, op-ed pieces, of every time Baldwin stood up in front of an audience—friendly or hostile—and said what he thought. "That's all there is," Baldwin wrote. "Only that work which is love and that love which is work will come anywhere obeying the dictum laid down by the great Ray Charles, and—tell the truth."[58]

Like many others, I added statements about #BlackLives-Matter to all my social media after the murder of George Floyd. Millions of people marched in BLM rallies. Others wrote op-ed pieces or contacted their legislators. Some of us had hard conversations with people who didn't believe as we do—or hard conversations with people on the other side of an identity divide. Seeing and speaking the truth matters.

Baldwin's agent in the early 1960s—the pinnacle of Baldwin's fame—warned him against taking too many speaking gigs. It seemed like only a day, he told Baldwin, but it's always days on either side, and preparation, and all of that takes you away from your central task of writing.[59] But Baldwin would have said that he had more than one central task. "The conflict," as he understood it, "was simply between my life as a writer and my life as—not spokesman, exactly, but as public witness to the situation of black people. I had to play both roles: there was nothing anyone, including myself, could do about it."[60]

I was once asked by a FOX News reporter why I felt it was important to speak out about racism—the implication being that since I'm a white, middle-class, middle-aged male, why don't I just sit in my comfortable home and do my comfortable job and not worry about things that don't affect me?

Because, I told her, James Baldwin and Martin Luther King Jr. and my Christian beliefs argue that when anyone is suffering, it is a matter of suffering for all of us. At the end of one of his most hopeless essays, *The Evidence of Things Not Seen*, written late in his life, Baldwin nonetheless came back to bearing witness to our interconnectedness. In his early years in the church, Baldwin (and I) had studied Scripture: "I had been told to *love everybody*. Whoever else did not believe this, I did." And Baldwin spoke of "the meaning of the word community: which, as I have understood it, simply means our endless connection with, and responsibility for, each other."[61]

This leaning into community means that we need to be in relationship, because only in relationship are we confronted, challenged, and encouraged to move forward. We learn from each other, if we are willing to listen. I still remember the first time I ever talked with Kelly Brown Douglas about her son Desmond, about how even though Desmond is a full-grown man, she still worries about his safety every time he leaves the house. I had known from my reading about police violence and public lynchings of Black men—but Kelly's love and dread brought the truth home to me in a way that mere facts could not, and I remain grateful for the challenge and opportunity our friendship has offered.

I remember an early conversation with Anthony Reddie, a great theologian working at Oxford, and likewise a great lover of James Baldwin. He talked about how odd it was to be a Black theologian fighting for liberation at the heart of the empire; it would not have occurred to me until he spoke it, since almost everyone around Oxford looked like me. In conversation and on social media, he has shared some of the travails of simply occupying a Black body: "I find myself reflecting on the continued complexities of living in a Black body. The bounded ways our bodies are marked ... No wonder so many of us suffer disproportionately from various forms of mental ill health."[62] Again: I have read about this problem, thought about it, but because I don't live with the reality of racism directed against those in Black bodies, I need to hear how it harms people I love and respect for the issues to truly come alive for me—and remain alive long enough to challenge me and to force me to work for change.

Baldwin knew that human beings do not necessarily like to be challenged. That we fear change. In *The Fire Next Time*, he pointed out that white Christians and the Nation of Islam both live behind the same set of myths, the same unthinking hatreds. The notion that they would talk across that divide—or that we would, for we live in a country that now is laced with vertiginous canyons—is at the heart of whether we can move forward. Conversation and relationship truly matter. A few years ago I wrote a book with the former archbishop of Canterbury, Rowan Williams. In it, Rowan said that one of the great gifts of our hours of conversation was that he hadn't always known what he believed until we talked about it. To engage a separate human being—one with different opinions, fears, hopes—in conversation is a necessary piece of the act of conversion. We can only change our minds when we are confronted by contradictory ideas, when we are pushed and challenged, and when we are affirmed that change is necessary.

This brings us back, at last, to Baldwin's meeting with RFK, and to other moments in his life we have seen. We recall Baldwin's debate with William F. Buckley; Buckley was not, apparently, convicted about the wrongness of his ideas, but the white rulers of the empire in attendance at the Cambridge Union listened to Baldwin with rapt attention, and when he finished, they offered him a standing ovation—recognition and, perhaps to some extent, relationship. Baldwin's words and presence had shaken and shaped them.

We remember Baldwin's encounters with Black artists and leaders, some of whom he loved and respected, some of whom he was in conflict with, some who fell into both categories—

Richard Wright, Malcolm X, Martin Luther King Jr., Medgar Evers, Elijah Muhammad, Eldridge Cleaver—and his attempts to listen and learn from them what he could as he formulated his own path forward.

And we think about his insistence that he was put on earth to be a witness: to tell his story and the story of others whose lives touched his so that the world might know, repent, and change.

Dr. King used to say that we are bound in a great web of mutuality—that injustice anywhere is injustice everywhere. So it is that relationship becomes a central part of progress. When I imagine Bobby Kennedy, angrily beset by a room full of Black people fed up with excuses and tired of geological change, I see a person very much like an earlier version of myself. White, sympathetic, and ignorant. More than once in the last half dozen years, I have been schooled about race by a person of color. Many of those people, thankfully, forgave my ignorance and remain my friends, and those relationships have taught me not only about their lived experiences but about my own, have sharpened my sense of how we might proceed together, and have inspired me to work on their behalf, as well as on my own.

Which brings us to repair. Some people like the word "reconciliation," which is a beautiful biblical concept; the Apostle Paul speaks about how followers of Jesus are called to be agents of reconciliation, which is a thing I hold dear: "All this is from God, who reconciled us to himself through Christ and has given us the ministry of reconciliation."[63] But some folks I admire greatly say we can't speak of reconciliation between whites and Blacks in America because there has never been connection. Some of my friends use the term "racial healing," and others speak about "reparations," a word that has some charged connotations.

But at heart, it is all about repair: How do we approach four hundred years of hatred, violence, suffering, and degradation and seek to make it better? To make America more just? To, as John Kennedy said, wonder "whether all Americans are to be afforded equal rights and equal opportunities, whether we are going to treat our fellow Americans as we want to be treated"?

Baldwin's conclusions here find him wrestling. It was indeed possible, he said, that white Americans had been white too long. That they might not want to give up their privilege. This is the Baldwin who feared that "it is not even remotely possible for the excluded to become the included, for this inclusion means, precisely, the end of the status quo."[64] And the status quo does not like to be changed, or, rather, those who benefit from it do not want it to change.

This process, as I suggested earlier, requires of white people something we might call repentance, although Baldwin used the equally powerful word "atonement": "If I were still in the pulpit which some people (and they may be right) claim I never left, I would counsel my countrymen to the self-confrontation of prayer, the cleansing breaking of the heart that precedes atonement. This is, of course, impossible. Multitudes are capable of many things, but atonement is not one of them."[65]

Perhaps multitudes can't. But individuals can, and must. And multitudes are made up of changed individuals, of those whose hearts have been broken but who are in the process of reassembling them. In this is our hope.

Baldwin called himself an optimist on that long-ago program with Kenneth Clark directly after their failed encounter with Bobby Kennedy: "I can't be a pessimist because I'm alive. To be a pessimist means that you have agreed that human life is an academic matter, so I'm forced to be an optimist. I'm forced to believe that we can survive whatever we must survive."[66] He argued then—as he did elsewhere for decades—that the future of America was precisely as bright as the future of Black people in America. That we would rise or fall together. And that meant, against all odds, that we might see change, that Baldwin, even in one of his final books, could still lean into the possibility of hope:

> This is the only nation under heaven that contains the universe—east and west, north and south, black and white. This is the only nation in the world that can hope to liberate—to begin to liberate—mankind from the strangling ideas of the national identity and the tyranny of the territorial dispute. I know this sounds remote now, and that I will not live to see anything resembling this hope come to pass. Yet I know that I *have* seen it—in fire and blood and anguish, true, but I have seen it. I speak with the authority of the slave born in the country once believed to be: *the last best hope of earth.*[67]

Witness and truth; community and love; recognition and relationship; repentance and atonement; commitment and hope. Nobody said this would be easy. Baldwin clawed his way back to optimism because where there is life, there is hope. But all of us can lean into his hope as well. If we're willing to grapple with our history, if we're willing to build relationships, to love against the grain, there is every possibility that, as Baldwin put it, we can make change: "At the bottom of my heart … I know that people can be better than they are."[68]

May it be so—for our sakes, and for those yet to come.

Baldwin on Justice

Is there not one righteous among them?

—James Baldwin,
from an unpublished draft of *Once When I Was Lost*

In our exploration of racial oppression earlier in this book, we made a turn, whether you realized it or not, toward the hope of realizing racial justice. Baldwin, who observed racial injustice in Paris, in his native Harlem, in his visits to the American South, and in cities across this country, thought, wrote, spoke, and marched as a witness to it, but he was also aware that racial injustice is only a subset of the inequities in our nation and the world.

Racial injustice is connected to other forms of unfairness. In his writing and other work, my friend Vann Newkirk II chronicles the ways being a person of color is connected to greater political injustice, health and climate inequities, legal miseries, and economic disparities. Poor whites have also been brutally victimized or marginalized by those with power and wealth (at the same time that they have been encouraged to take comfort in racist notions that because of the color of their skin they're still superior to those darker than themselves). Baldwin worked against all of these forms of injustice because, at the end of the day, what he was seeking for himself and the rest of the human family was simple human justice: all of us deserve equity, dignity, and freedom.

I suspect Baldwin was tied up in questions of justice from an early age, for children—as I well know, having parented a few—are very conscious of the concept of fairness: *is somebody being treated more or less well than I am?* The concept of fairness is something we feel keenly in childhood. Baldwin knew early on that he was the object of his father's loathing, a lightning rod for his father's misery. He said of his father, "He could be chilling in the pulpit and indescribably cruel in his personal life and he was certainly the most bitter man I have ever met." He wrote that his father "flew into a rage" and conjured up "the most appalling scenes."[1] His father's violence and cruelty grew out of his own brokenness, but Baldwin must have understood early on that the way they broke against his flesh and soul were not prompted by his own failings: they were unfair and unjust, even though David Baldwin was his father.

Baldwin also talks about how he became aware from early life that the color of his skin meant certain things about his reality: that he was imprisoned in a ghetto, that he had comparatively limited opportunities for education and later advancement, that representatives of the law took an especial interest in him despite his innocence. In *The Fire Next Time*, Baldwin spoke of "the incessant and gratuitous humiliation and danger one encountered every working day, all day long"—of how when he was ten, he was frisked, humiliated, and left flat on his back in a vacant lot by two white policemen; how when he was thirteen, a policeman on Fifth Avenue muttered at him as he crossed the street to the main branch of the New York Public Library, "Why don't you niggers stay uptown where you belong?"[2]

Baldwin knew—as so many know—that this treatment is unfair and unjust. That it is not merited. That, in a word, it is wicked:

> The brutality with which Negroes are treated in this country cannot be overstated, however unwilling white men may be to hear it. In the beginning—and neither can this be overstated—a Negro just cannot *believe* that white people are treating him as they do; he does not know what he has done to merit it. And when he realizes that the treatment accorded him has nothing to do with anything that he has done, that the attempt of white people to destroy him—for that is what it is—is utterly gratuitous, it is hard not to think of white people as devils.[3]

In *Go Tell It on the Mountain*, Florence's mother is one of many Black characters who imagines that God will respond to the wicked and uplift the righteous: "She did not forget that deliverance was promised and would surely come. She had only to endure and trust in God. . . . She told her children, God was just."[4] The justice of God—particularly when delayed or seemingly misapplied—occupied Baldwin's thoughts throughout his life. Religious people in Baldwin's works often consult their beliefs about God to explain why wickedness happens to good people, to express where God is in the middle of pain and injustice.

Those explanations are often singularly unhelpful. In *The Amen Corner*, Mrs. Jackson, who has recently lost a baby, comes to Sister Margaret and lets loose her grief—"Ain't nobody ever done nothing bad enough to suffer like that baby suffered." Like other characters in the play, she observes that some events don't seem just or right: "I been trying to pray. Every time I kneel down, I see my baby again—and—I can't pray."[5] The impulse behind this scene—and of others in the play—is not that God is directly causing these horrors, but that suffering is a reality and must be borne in this world.

The Rev. Meridian Henry, father of the murdered Richard in *Blues for Mister Charlie*, is also working his way toward some theological insights into the evil that men do and where God is—or isn't—in those acts: "What was the sin committed by our forefathers ... which has had to be expiated by chains, by the lash, by hunger and thirst, by slaughter, by fire, by the rope, by the knife, and for so many generations, on these wild shores, in this strange land?"[6] As with Mrs. Jackson, the wickedness ultimately is not the product of cosmic unfairness; the condition of the formerly enslaved in a town that Baldwin refers to in the introduction to the play as "Plaguetown, USA" is a product of human wickedness, not of God's indifference or injustice.[7]

Finally, Baldwin also would have been familiar with biblical teachings on justice and righteousness, concepts that are directly linked in both the Hebrew Bible and the Christian Testament. He knew the Bible as a young preacher and referenced it throughout his life, including the epigraph for this chapter I discovered in Harlem in a draft of his screenplay *One Day When I Was Lost,* and the similar passage some years later from the end of *If Beale Street Could Talk*. Tish, who is very pregnant at this point in the story, says,

> *From my chair, I looked out my window, over these*
>   *dreadful streets.*
> *The baby asked,*
> *Is there not one righteous among them?*

This despairing phrase feels biblical because it echoes biblical passages. In the King James translation Baldwin knew and imbibed, we find this in the wisdom book of Ecclesiastes: "For there is not a just man upon earth, that doeth good, and sinneth not."[8] Baldwin also might have had in mind a debate between Abraham and God in Genesis 18 about whether God should destroy the sinful cities of the plain, Sodom and Gomorrah:

> And the men turned their faces from thence, and went toward Sodom: but Abraham stood yet before the LORD.
> And Abraham drew near, and said, Wilt thou also destroy the righteous with the wicked?
> Peradventure there be fifty righteous within the city: wilt thou also destroy and not spare the place for the fifty righteous that are therein?
> That be far from thee to do after this manner, to slay the righteous with the wicked: and that the righteous should be as the wicked, that be far from thee: Shall not the Judge of all the earth do right?
> And the Lord said, If I find in Sodom fifty righteous within the city, then I will spare all the place for their sakes.[9]

Ultimately Abraham bargains the Lord down to agreeing that God will spare the cities if ten righteous people can be found there (spoiler alert: they can't), and by extrapolation we might think that if there were a single righteous human among them, perhaps God would spare the city.

But what do we make of this term "righteous"? I am fond of the song "I Am a Patriot," a modern spiritual written and initially recorded by Steven Van Zandt and covered by Jackson

Browne, the Burns Sisters, and Pearl Jam, a song that centers on the fight for justice, not for political or personal gain: "And the river opens for the righteous." For many of us, the word "righteous" has the smack of religious faith about it, and you might rightly argue that we have already focused on James Baldwin's thoughts on religion and faith (and so we have, although you're already seeing how difficult it can be to segregate the interconnected concerns of a great artist's work and life). But the Hebrew word *tzedek*, which is sometimes translated in the Bible as "righteousness," is another of those words with nuance; it's important for us to consider it carefully.

In the Hebrew prophetic tradition of Jeremiah, Amos, Micah, and others, faith should lead to justice: God asks both of us. But the "justice" that the Hebrew Bible leans into is positive behavior, not simply punishment. If you open *The Oxford Companion to the Bible* and flip to the entry on "Justice" you discover this: "Justice. *See* Righteousness." This shouldn't surprise us, since the word *tzedek* is used for justice and righteousness. It's a word that describes all of righteous life under God, what we are called to do as well as what we are supposed to shun.[10] The Bible is full of these teachings about how righteousness and justice are intertwined, how in this call for righteous persons we are actually offering a call for greater justice from and for all. A city without righteous persons in it is riddled with corruption and cruelty; a nation where the needs of the marginalized are swept aside and the desires of the rich and powerful are always kept top of mind is unjust.

Remember the Temple Sermon from Jeremiah, the Hebrew prophet with whom Baldwin most of all identified, which we quoted earlier? It was given to privileged people who thought that right prayer and right worship—outward and simple signs of righteousness—were God's desire. But what Jeremiah said is that worship and belief mean nothing without a commitment to those who are suffering injustice. A few chapters later, that same prophet leans deeper into discussion about righteousness and the necessity for rulers and subjects—for all people—to engage in it:

> Thus says the Lord: Go down to the house of the king of Judah, and speak there this word, and say: Hear the word of the Lord, O king of Judah sitting on the throne of David—you, and your servants, and your people who enter these gates. Thus says the Lord: Act with justice and righteousness and deliver from the hand of the oppressor anyone who has been robbed. And do no wrong or violence to the alien, the orphan, and the widow, or shed innocent blood in this place. For if you will indeed obey this word, then through the gates of this house shall enter kings who sit on the throne of David, riding in chariots and on horses—they, their servants, and their people. But if you will not heed these words, I swear by myself, says the Lord, that this house shall become a desolation.[11]

Biblical scholar John M. Bracke, reflecting on this section of Jeremiah, notes how it clearly calls for the king/ruler/government to administer justice, and how Jeremiah "identifies the substance of justice to be the protection of the weaker members of society from oppression by those more powerful."[12] It is a concern throughout Jeremiah, a calling for everyone in the society, "rich and poor, common citizen or monarch alike" to seek equity and fairness for all, with that failure leading to what should now be familiar language from Jeremiah 5:

> *Run to and fro through the streets of Jerusalem,*
>   *look around and take note!*
> *Search its squares and see*
>   *if you can find one person*
> *who acts justly*
>   *and seeks truth—*
> *so that I may pardon Jerusalem.*[13]

Is there not one righteous among them?

In *The Evidence of Things Not Seen*, Baldwin takes up Jeremiah's argument that all of us bear a responsibility to act justly: "It's impossible to pretend that you are not heir to, and therefore, however inadequately and unwillingly, responsible to, and for, the time and place that give you life—without becoming, at very best, a dangerously disoriented human being."[14] Like Jeremiah, he says there is judgment for failing to be righteous.

My friend the Rev. Dr. Hulitt Gloer, a white Baptist pastor and former professor of preaching at Baylor's Truett Theological Seminary, wrote me when he learned I was preparing a chapter on Baldwin's teachings on justice and righteousness. As you'd expect from a Bible scholar and preacher, Hulitt also dug deeply into Scripture and into interpretation to consider the topic, offering this advice:

Righteousness in the Gospel of Matthew can be summed up as "doing the will of God" or "fulfilling God's purposes." The Greek word for "righteousness" can also be translated "justice." Thus, doing justice, whoever is doing it and wherever it is being done, is doing the will of God, fulfilling God's purposes. The Old Testament summary is Micah 6:8 ["He has told you, O mortal, what is good, / and what does the Lord require of you / but to do justice and to love kindness / and to walk humbly with your God?"]. In the NT, it's the great commandment explained in Matthew 5:43–48 ["love your enemies"], the Good Samaritan, and Matthew 25:31–46 [the "righteous" are those who feed the hungry, visit those imprisoned, care for the sick]. I'm sure this is nothing new to you, but it seems to me that Baldwin's work was all about justice, and as such, intentionally or not, he was about God's work of justice.[15]

Justice and righteousness are indeed the goals and Baldwin's great desires, and we will talk more about that, believe me, but to understand these positive workings fully, we have to apprehend how hard they are to get to, how difficult this world—and, in particular, this country—make it to do the right thing. Baldwin, in prophetic passages in *No Name in the Street*, used the very biblical word "wickedness" as an antonym for "righteousness," and one can almost hear the judgment of Jeremiah in the Temple as Baldwin offers these words: "One sees that most human beings are wretched, and, in one way or another, become wicked." Later, prompted by a journey into the heart of darkness, the American South, Baldwin returned to this topic: "As social and moral and political and sexual entities, white Americans are probably the sickest and certainly the most dangerous people ... to be found in the world today.... I was not struck by their wickedness, for that wickedness was but the spirit and the history of America."[16]

Baldwin's books and talks bear witness to that spirit and history of white American wickedness and could lead us into a discussion of what the word "justice" means for us, what it often means in the Bible, and what it sometimes meant in Baldwin's discourse: punitive or retributive justice. Justice in our culture is typically about crime and punishment: the Justice League, the justice system, *Law and Order*. We are punished for our wrong actions, whether by God or the courts, or perhaps by those we have wronged. It is human nature and human hope to believe that wickedness will receive its just reward, even though it often does not—even though, in what feels like the rankest injustice, the innocent are often punished instead of the guilty, or the guilty go free.

In the biblical examples we've so far seen, there is typically a carrot-and-stick construction: the righteous will gain certain blessings, and the unrighteous will be justly punished. In the example of Abraham lobbying for the Cities of the Plain, for example, his advocacy concerns whether he might dissuade God's judgment, the complete and utter destruction of Sodom and Gomorrah (spoiler alert: he doesn't). In the Temple Sermon in Jeremiah, the flipside of the reward for those who are righteous ("I will dwell with you in this place") is a punishment for those who ignore the Word of the Lord, for those who sacrifice to other gods from the high places of Topheth in the valley of the son of Hinnom:

> Therefore the days are surely coming, says the Lord, when it will no more be called Topheth or the valley of the son of Hinnom but the valley of Slaughter, for they will bury in Topheth until there is no more room. The corpses of this people will be food for the birds of the air and for the animals of the earth, and no one will frighten them away. And I will bring to an end the sound of mirth and gladness, the voice of the bride and bridegroom in the cities of Judah and in the streets of Jerusalem, for the land shall become a waste.[17]

It does not sound good for the wicked, and this is a remarkably gruesome but typical example of the sort of punitive justice represented throughout the Scriptures. Individual sinners are cast into outer darkness, where there is weeping and gnashing of teeth.[18] Unjust nations and societies are brought to ruin, an object of horror, a proverb, and a byword among all the peoples where the Lord leads them.[19] The sense in the Scriptures is that justice will prevail, even if in the present moment things look dark. Perhaps this is why Dr. King repeated in his last sermon, delivered at Washington's National Cathedral, words he had often used: "We shall overcome because the arc of the moral universe is long but it bends toward justice."[20]

The difficulty—and the greatest injustice—emerges when justice seems to miscarry on some cosmic level. The guilty escape judgment, which is visited instead upon those who do not deserve it, something Jeremiah and Baldwin both witnessed and wrote about. Judgment is often, as Baldwin observed, directed against those who cannot easily defend themselves against it—the poor, minorities, the marginalized, and the powerless. It can even feel, as Reverend Henry speculates in *Blues for Mister Charlie*, that maybe the Eyes of God are blind, so blind does justice sometimes seem.[21]

This is a theme in Baldwin's work from early on, for he had in his childhood in America, and later in France, personally been a victim of this sort of blind justice. In the essay "Equal in Paris," Baldwin describes the Kafkaesque experience of being thrown into a French jail in 1949 for receiving stolen property from an acquaintance: a bedsheet a friend had taken in a fit of petulance from his hotel when leaving it. "When he arrived at my hotel I borrowed the sheet," Baldwin says, "because my own were filthy and the chambermaid showed no signs of bringing me any clean ones."[22] When the French police arrived to inves-tigate the matter of the stolen bedsheet, they discovered it in on Baldwin's bed and took both him and his friend into custody. Baldwin describes his battle to control his panic "in a country I knew nothing about, in the hands of a people I did not under-stand at all.... It was quite clear to me that the Frenchmen in whose hands I found myself were no better or worse than their American counterparts. Certainly their uniforms frightened me quite as much, and their impersonality, and the threat, always very keenly felt by the poor, of violence, was as present in that commissariat as it had ever been for me in any police station."[23] Baldwin had seen the violence the French police were capable of in their treatment of Black Algerians, and he always felt his American passport was perhaps the lone thing keeping him from similar damage.

He was handcuffed, transported in a terrifying paddy wagon, fingerprinted, and photographed. He spent days—including Christmas Day—in a cold cell with a central hole for a toilet shared with his cellmates: old men who seemed barely alive, career criminals, North Africans "who seemed the only living people in this place because they yet retained the grace to be bewildered."[24] In the paddy wagon taking him from the jail to prison, Baldwin broke down, weeping through the whole trip to Fresnes, a prison where during World War II the Gestapo tortured—and even executed—captured British agents and members of the French Resistance. It was not then (and is not now) a nice place. It is stunning to imagine the slight, thoughtful, dazed Baldwin dumped in such a place, "divested of shoelaces, belt, watch, money, papers, nailfile, in a freezing cell in which both the window and the toilet were broken, with six other adventurers" who heard his tale of the bedsheet ("*l'affaire du drap de lit*") with either wild amusement or "suspicious disbelief." His companions took their imprisonment as "another unlucky happening in a very dirty world," and on reflection, Baldwin realized that "they were far more realistic about the world than I, and more nearly right about it."[25]

Baldwin's long ordeal might not have had an end if one of his cellmates had not been acquitted and asked each of his cellmates if they had anyone on the outside to whom they'd like him to carry a message. Baldwin, after first saying no, asked the man to notify an American patent attorney in whose office Baldwin had clerked. That attorney got a trial lawyer for Baldwin and appeared as a character witness for him, and on December 27, the charges against Baldwin and his friend were dismissed. What Baldwin took away from that experience—those days in bleak French jails and prisons when he was guilty of nothing more dramatic than sleeping on a stolen bedsheet—was the laughter in the courtroom when *l'affaire du drap de lit* was brought up. He described it as chilling: "the laughter of those who consider themselves to be at a safe remove from all the wretched, for whom the pain of living is not real." It was the laughter of those who could not imagine the human consequences of injustice—or even the very real suffering of those undergoing deserved punishments. Baldwin resolved that he would not forget that this laughter, which he thought perhaps he had left behind in America, "is universal and never can be stilled."[26]

Baldwin did not forget about this miscarriage of justice. Indeed, how could he, when he witnessed many more and much worse during the course of his life? His questioning of punitive justice, of its potential to ensnare, damage, and even destroy the innocent, comes out in both fiction and nonfiction, beginning with a crucial scene toward the end of *Go Tell It on the Mountain*, his first novel. In a section where the narration turns away from the primary character, John Grimes, to explore the lives and backstories of John's mother, aunt, and adoptive father, "Elizabeth's Prayer," it circles in on the story of John's mother and biological father, Richard.

When Richard doesn't show up for an appointment, Elizabeth goes looking for him. Although she is pregnant with Richard's child, she has not told him yet, a decision she regrets. His landlady tells her that he hasn't been home for several days, and then two white policemen show up and tell them that Richard is in jail for "robbing a white man's store."

Richard hasn't robbed anyone, she tells them. She knows he is incapable of such a thing. All the same, one of the police officers replies callously, insisting that her boyfriend is guilty without question, and that he's headed to jail for it.[27]

Elizabeth's experience at the police station is full of injustice and brutality—officers ask inappropriate questions about her relationship with Richard, proposition her—and she "felt that she was about to burst, or vomit, or die. . . . She felt herself, from every side, being covered with a stink and filth."[28] When she finally gets to him, she weeps. He has been beaten so badly he can barely walk. He did not, of course, leave her apartment late at night and rob a store; he was standing on the subway platform when he encountered three Black men pursued by the police and is taken to the station house with them. Although they corroborate his story—he was not one of them—when the store owner comes to identify the culprits, he names all four of them.

Even though Richard shouts that it wasn't him, insisting that the shop owner look at him and really see who he is—not someone who has done him wrong—the man replies, "You black bastards, you're all the same."[29]

When Richard is taken to prison awaiting his trial, Elizabeth can't believe the injustice of the system, of the world—although also, she can, because she has always known it. She cannot think of one righteous white person in the whole world, and she can only think about the day when divine justice might redress this: "She hoped that one day, God, with tortures inconceivable, would grind them utterly into humility, and make them know that black boys and black girls, whom they treated with such condescension, such disdain, and such good humor, had hearts like human beings, too, more human hearts than theirs."[30]

Richard, like Baldwin himself, is ultimately released. He does not serve a long sentence. But unlike Baldwin, what Richard has experienced breaks him utterly. This young Black man—who does not and will never know that he is John's father—throws himself on his bed and weeps. Elizabeth holds him as he shakes violently.[31]

That night, Richard commits suicide. And while Elizabeth goes on, gives birth to John, later marries her friend Florence's brother Gabriel, fresh in the North after the death of his wife, initially she thinks of her old self as buried with Richard, and her survival is a slow, hard thing: "She knew through what fires the soul must crawl, and with what weeping one passed over."[32]

Baldwin's life was marked by the suicides, murders, early deaths, and unfair incarceration of many friends and acquaintances. In 1974 he told *The Guardian*, "I'm 49 years old, and I have no old friends."[33] By 1974 Baldwin had seen the assassinations of Dr. King and Malcolm X—both marked by significant mysteries and conspiracies—and Medgar Evans, a good man killed in Mississippi by the white supremacist Byron De La Beckwith, who because of witnesses who perjured themselves and biased jury selections escaped judgment in two trials that ended in hung juries.[34] Baldwin would not live to see him finally convicted in 1994, so as with these other deaths, Baldwin knew only the injustice and the failure of justice connected with them.

Perhaps the accusation did not surprise him when he heard that his friend Tony Maynard was accused of killing a white Marine with a shotgun in New York City. The surprise came because, just as Elizabeth knew Richard had not robbed any store, Baldwin knew that Tony would not have been involved in the sordid events that led to the Marine being shot and that Tony would never have used so inelegant a weapon as a sawed-off shotgun.[35] Tony and Baldwin had been close—Tony had been Baldwin's bodyguard, chauffeur, and administrative assistant—and although they grew apart because Tony felt that the civil rights movement was elitist, Baldwin did not hesitate for a moment when he heard that Tony had been incarcerated in Germany, and that he was expected to be extradited to America to stand trial.

With the help of his German publishers, Baldwin arranged to visit Tony in prison, although it was surely a terrifying reminder of his past experiences and he remembered all those symbolized by Richard who were broken by the system. "I was frightened," he says of visiting the prison, "in a way very hard to describe. The fact that this was the fabled Germany of the Third Reich, and this was a German prison, certainly had something to do with it. I was not so much afraid to see him as I was afraid of what might have happened to him—in him. . . . One does not know what is left of the person. Human help often arrives too late, and if the person has really turned his face to the wall, no human being can help."[36]

Baldwin was relieved to see that Tony had not yet turned his face to the wall, and in their first conversation Baldwin became more and more convinced of Tony's innocence and the rank injustice of the situation. In order to believe any of the prosecution's assertions, he said, "It would be necessary to invent a Tony whom no one knew. But that, of course, would pose no difficulty for the police or the jury or the judge."[37]

In *No Name in the Street*, Baldwin recalls another Black friend who told him about how he was treated by the police simply because he was dating a white woman. One day, one of those officers saw him alone on the street and told him, "I'm going to get you." Baldwin's friend told him that he "started dreaming about that cop. He never spoke to me again, just looked at me like that every time we passed each other on the street. I knew he meant it. If I hung around too long, he'd find a way."[38]

Baldwin remembered his own experiences in New York, including how police used to egg on bystanders who cursed and spit on him when he walked with a white girl he knew in Greenwich Village, and how once a white woman he was sleeping with slapped his face in Washington Square Park and he had to flee for his life. Like his unnamed friend, like Tony, Baldwin says, "I was black and visible and helpless.... And the prisons of this country are full of boys like the boy I was."[39]

Baldwin swore on his soul to get Tony out. He paid lawyers and lent his celebrity to the cause. Tony wanted to fight the extradition process because, Baldwin says, "he was certain that he would be murdered on the way back home. This fear may strike the ordinary American as preposterous.... But I didn't find his terror ... in the least preposterous."[40] Baldwin wanted to fight the proceedings because he believed Tony should be regarded as a political prisoner. "I agree with the Black Panther position concerning black prisoners: not one of them has ever had a fair trial, for not one of them has ever been tried by a jury of his peers."[41]

Not that Germany was any more just; one evening Baldwin, his publisher, and the lawyer arrived to be told that they could not see Tony. The publisher told the prison employee that they were prepared to wait until morning—or forever. That they were not leaving until they saw him. At that, Tony was found and produced. He had been badly beaten and was weeping. "When I say that heads surely rolled and that someone had goofed," Baldwin says with what reads like controlled fury, "I do not mean that they goofed because they beat him. They goofed because they let us see him."[42]

Tony was extradited back to America to stand trial—despite Baldwin's best efforts—and at the writing of *No Name in the Street*, Baldwin announced that "Tony has been in prison since October 27, 1967, and remains in prison still."[43] This disheartening result was despite Tony being championed by one of America's best-known writers, despite the resources that Baldwin provided, the expensive defense attorneys he retained. The obvious conclusion is that for those without such capabilities—those boys like Baldwin once was—the desperation and terror would be even greater.

After two failed trials, Tony was convicted in 1970 of first-degree manslaughter and sentenced to ten to twenty years in prison. Then, on a judge's order in 1974, he was set free. The *New York Times* reported that "William A. (Tony) Maynard was freed on bail yesterday after six and a half years in jails in Germany and the United States for a crime he has steadfastly maintained he did not commit, and when he walked out of a State Supreme Court hearing, his knees momentarily buckled." It will not perhaps surprise you that just as Byron De La Beckwith's defense was abetted by fraud and dishonesty, in Tony's case, "the prosecution had 'suppressed' critical information about a witness."[44] The Manhattan district attorney dismissed the case later that year, and Tony was—and remains—a free man, no thanks to a system that preferred finding a culprit and not *the* culprit—and that, like the shop owner in *Go Tell It on the Mountain* as much as said, "You Black bastards, you're all alike."

The story that underlies *If Beale Street Could Talk*—that Fonny is falsely accused of a crime because of a vindictive police officer and an unstable witness, yet languishes in prison—clearly comes from Baldwin's friendship with and advocacy for Tony Maynard. Maynard's lawyer Lewis M. Steel told *TIME* magazine that "his client, like Fonny, had been 'up against a system that cared little about guilt or innocence' and that Baldwin had been 'well aware' of the situation." Tony Maynard, for his part, simply said that "of course" *Beale Street* was inspired by his travails and Baldwin's close connection to them.

If Beale Street Could Talk (adapted in 2018 by Oscar-winner Barry Jenkins, who calls Baldwin his "personal school of life") represents the artistic culmination of Baldwin's sad and angry indictment of a punitive justice system that sometimes harms those caught up in it more than it helps to create a just society.[45] It explores Fonny's story largely through those who love him, showing the ripple effects of how a corrupt system hurts everyone connected to one falsely imprisoned. Tish, Fonny's lover, is the primary narrator of the book, the "central consciousness" (as Henry James, whom Baldwin admired, would call it) through whom the novel's action is filtered. When a Puerto Rican woman is raped far from where Fonny lives, a police officer nonetheless testifies that it was Fonny who did it, and the woman—who has never before seen Fonny—nonetheless is induced to identify him as the assailant, and he is held over for trial. Then follows Fonny's imprisonment, his and her family's attempts to get him released, and their despair, anger, and hope are mostly represented in her words, memories, and emotions.

Black and Brown people make up most of those incarcerated around Fonny, and late in the novel, Tish's mother, who has gone to Puerto Rico to talk with the victim, concludes, "I don't speak no Spanish and they don't speak no English.... We on the same garbage dump. For the same reason.... I had never thought about it like that before. Who*ever* discovered America *deserved* to be dragged home, in chains, to die."[46]

What happens to Fonny and all who love him is also an injustice. Early in the novel, Tish says of a visit to Fonny, "I hope that nobody has ever had to look at anybody they love through glass."[47] Because of the brilliant use of Tish as a filter character, readers and viewers are invited to identify with this pain and heartbreak and imagine what they might do in the face of some similar injustice. Tish realizes she would be willing to sell herself to get money for Fonny's defense; her mother goes to Puerto Rico hoping to convince the victim that she has made a mistake; Tish's and Fonny's fathers break the law in order to raise the funds to pay Fonny's lawyer.

Fonny comes to some conclusions about American justice—or the perversion of it—toward the end. He is not in jail for anything he has done: "These captive men are the hidden price for a hidden lie: the righteous must be able to locate the damned." Fonny understands how things work now, and he is resolved: they are not going to destroy him, regardless of their power. As Tish realizes, Fonny is fighting for his life—and fighting to be around when his baby is born.[48]

One last example of Baldwin struggling with the injustice of the justice system comes in *The Evidence of Things Not Seen*. While he again acknowledges how closely linked racism and injustice are in the specific topic of his writing—the Atlanta child murders and the young Black man who was convicted of them—he is also well aware of how economic justice (or injustice) factors into laws that go on the books, into civic policies, into policing and criminal justice policies. Atlanta has liked to tout itself as an economic powerhouse, the city too busy to hate. Yet Baldwin discovers there may be plenty of hate there after all.

Former Atlanta mayor and civil rights icon Andrew Young, who took office just after the string of murders, argues that the slogan meant and maybe still means something: "And it was understood that Atlanta was about business. It didn't have time for racism and for keeping anybody down. It was a city that was supposedly lifting everybody up."[49] Atlanta pointed to its prosperous Black middle class and professionals; unlike Tulsa and other places in America, this successful Black community was not burned to the ground. Today, you can still go see the neighborhood where Martin Luther King Jr. grew up, see how with one obvious exception he lived a life that seems similar to that of white middle-class children.

The exception, of course, is that it was a Black neighborhood, separated from white neighborhoods by white design.

Baldwin questioned the myth of Black affluence and the idea that successful Blacks refute the nation's notions that racism is still a powerful force. He also discussed the importance of wealth, and how that word means a whole lot more than we think it means:

> Wealth is not the same thing as affluence. Wealth, that is, is not the power to buy, but the power to dictate the terms of that so magical marketplace—or at the very least, to influence those terms. Wealth is the power to influence or to change the city's zoning laws or the insurance rates, or the actuarial tables they apply to Blacks or the textbook industry or the father-to-son labor unions or the composition of grand juries and the boards of education. Wealth is the power to make one's needs felt and to force a response to these needs.[50]

Yes, racism was and is a factor in the injustice Baldwin witnessed and wrote about, and it still is. The *British Medical*

Journal, reporting on a study from 2015 to 2020, announced that Black, Indigenous, and Latinx Americans were much more likely to be killed by police officers than white people. The study concludes, "Our findings suggest the influence of an insidious anti-Black and anti-Indigenous logic to police violence that warrants further exploration into the role of these factors in fatal police encounters."[51] Despite the monumental Black Lives Matter rallies across the country and around the world that followed George Floyd's murder in 2020, statistics show that Black people continue to experience a much greater risk of encountering lethal force.[52]

In *The Evidence of Things Not Seen*, Baldwin laid this great risk at the feet of racism and white supremacy: "Most White North Americans are always lying to, and concerning, their darker brother, which means they are always lying to themselves. Who doubts me has only to consider the state of the Union."[53]

Barry Jenkins, in adapting *Beale Street*, expressed a similar message about racism and its unchanging role in perpetuating injustice and malfeasance in an interview with *TIME*'s Eliza Berman:

> "It seemed to me there was an implicit power in allowing [the film] to remain set in the early 1970s," he says, "and to illustrate how pervasive these problems have been and how little we've done to correct them." Might that lead audiences to see the tale as squarely situated in the past tense? Sure, says Jenkins. But only if they haven't absorbed story after story of unarmed black men killed by police, not to mention untold others whose lives have been upended by the twin forces of structural racism and mass incarceration.[54]

But Baldwin, as ever, is clear that race is not the only injustice. His lucid discussion of the power of wealth to shape policies and control who wins, who loses, who gets away with things, and who gets blamed for things reminds us that economic inequities remain the constant reality. He knew, and often said, that poor white Americans had more in common with poor people of color than with those white men who were the fountains of industry and wolves of Wall Street, and he had a strange and almost preternatural sympathy for poor white racists like Lyle, the murderer in *Blues for Mister Charlie*. "If it is true, and I believe it is, that all men are brothers," he wrote in the published notes to the play, "then we have the duty to try to understand this wretched man; and while we probably cannot hope to liberate him, begin working toward the liberation of his children."[55]

Lyle has his own economic desperation, a sense of his own lack of power, and while none of that excuses his racist violence, Baldwin knew that Lyle was not inhuman. In his unpublished personal notes for the play, housed in the James Baldwin Papers at the Schomburg Center for Research in Black Culture in Harlem, Baldwin called for anyone interpreting the play to look for the Lyle in all of us. He saw Lyle as another example of that wretched American innocence, that he is, in a sense, the only innocent in the play. Lyle wears so many masks covering pain that he will not ever recognize. To give credence to that pain would destroy him. Pain causes him to lash out, not at the true sources of injustice, but at those over whom he has been taught to believe he still has power and can manifest status. Baldwin invests this poor white southern store owner with his own deep sympathies, even as he loathes the actions Lyle takes and the system that produced him and will protect him. Baldwin's conclusion is stunning: even though Lyle is the villain of *Blues for Mister Charlie*, you can't treat Lyle simply as a villain and hope to understand him.[56]

Racial injustice, legal injustice, economic injustice—Baldwin saw that these were and are and will always be intertwined. That these forces hold down people of color and people of all sorts who don't command wealth, people of every description who remain outside the centers of power and authority, that these forces cause all of those a disproportionate amount of suffering. This suffering can only happen for so long, of course. At some point, those people who have been held down for too long will rise up, or will rise up over and over again to secure their rights and their dignity. This was the great fear of slave owners like Thomas Jefferson: that the history of slave rebellions in Haiti and in the States might become America's reality. Jefferson clearly worried about what he called a "reversal of fortunes." He said that to be a slaveholder was like riding a "wolf [held] by the ears.... We can neither hold him nor safely let him go," and he lamented that even if emancipation were possible, whites had "deeply rooted prejudices," and Blacks "ten thousand recollections." The only possible end of such an uprising, he thought, would be the complete extermination of one race or the other.[57] This is the threatened judgment of *The Fire Next Time*, "the fulfillment of that prophecy, re-created from the Bible in song by a slave, is upon us: *God gave Noah the rainbow sign, No more water, the fire next time!*"[58] Justice will come, at last. And liberation will at last be real and complete.

During his lifetime, Baldwin saw African nations rise up and overthrow white colonial governments. He saw the Nation of Islam planning to push the white oppressors into the sea. He saw Black Panthers chanting, marching, fighting for Black Power.

Yet remarkably, from early in his life to the end of it, Baldwin continued to hold hope that the battle might be won without battle. In *Blues for Mister Charlie*, Reverend Henry insists that he doesn't want vengeance. He isn't even seeking punitive justice against Lyle, perhaps because he knows he will never see it. What he wants, he says, is simply to know the truth, if Lyle has indeed murdered his son, and for Lyle to face the evil of his actions square-on.[59] This is what Baldwin, with all of his talk of claiming and repenting of our history, his lamenting of white innocence and wishful naivete, also wants, what in fact the Bible prophets called for: turn from evil and do good.

Dr. King in Memphis the night before his murder spoke of how if he couldn't reach the promised land, at least he had been to the mountaintop and seen the other side. In an interview a few years before his death, in words that sound remarkably like King's, Baldwin was asked about his dreams and fantasies. A good dream, he said, was "that I am working for the New Jerusalem. That's true, I'm not joking. I won't live to see it, but I do believe in it. I think we're going to be better than we are."[60] As he said, the sum total of his wisdom was simply this: we can do better.

Change and real justice cannot be attained without arduous, backbreaking work, mind you, by any of us. You may have noticed we have not yet reached the New Jerusalem. Baldwin said that all Americans are standing in the same dark shadow, "a shadow which can only be lifted by human courage and honor."[61] In *Nobody Knows My Name,* he observes that whites cannot be free until they make the difficult decision to change: "It is only when a man is able, without bitterness or self-pity, to surrender a dream he has long cherished or a privilege he had long possessed that he is set free—he has set himself free—for higher dreams, for greater privileges."[62] Until persons recognize and lay down that privilege, true justice for all is impossible. Still, no one gets away with anything. That's the principle of higher justice and certainly Baldwin's own conclusion: "One cannot escape anything one has done. One has got to pay for it. You either pay for it willingly or pay for it unwillingly."[63] Perhaps one gives up one's privilege willingly, or that privilege can be wrested away unwillingly. One comes with less violence and toil.

Meanwhile, Baldwin said, Black people have the difficult task of recognizing that we are all bound up in our shared and corrosive history of American racial oppression. As Dagmawi Woubshet wrote in *The Atlantic* about *The Fire Next Time*, "Writing two years before the end of legal segregation, Baldwin demands black people not only to accept whites, but to do so *with love*, positioning black love as a vital instrument for white liberation and interracial renewal on a national scale."[64] It was a heroic task to ask of the oppressed—again, the words "human courage and honor" come to mind—but Baldwin had seen the end results of fear and hatred, and would have agreed with Dr. King's formulation that "darkness cannot drive out darkness; only light can do that. Hate cannot drive out hate; only love can do that."[65] Dr. King argued that what was required was the capacity to love, to love until the oppressor is humbled and brought to his knees.

You and I can express all our logical objections and suggest our reservations. Are all the oppressed—people of color, Indigenous people, poor people, LGBTQ people, immigrants and refugees—are they all called to love those in power who hate and despise them?

Is such magnanimity impossible?

Aren't those who are held down, murdered, spat upon literally and metaphorically, entitled to rise up and fight back?

Baldwin knew and saw what was happening around him wherever he went. He was a poor man taken to prison in Paris. He watched Black children spat upon in Arkansas and elsewhere. He saw Algerians beaten—and disappeared—in France.

If anyone had a right to give up hope, to call for violence, or to simply say that division was the way things had always been and the way they always would be, it was him. Yet that's not what we find him doing.

True, there were times in his life that were etched in despair. Baldwin has said that after Dr. King's death, for a time he couldn't write or hope. Reflecting on Dr. King's death and legacy, Baldwin said, "To look around the United States today is enough to make prophets and angels weep, and, certainly, the children's teeth are set on edge. This is not the land of the free, it is only very unwillingly and sporadically the home of the brave, and all that can be said for the bulk of our politicians is that, if they are no worse than they were, they are certainly no better."[66]

Yet at the end of *No Name in the Street*, Baldwin wrote that the old world was dying, and the new one, "kicking in the belly of its mother," announced that it is ready to be born.

In later interviews, he talked about how he had found it impossible to write after Dr. King's death—and how it was impossible not to. For Martin's sake—and his own, and the nation's—he picked up the work and kept hoping, as indeed he kept hoping to the end of his days.

A cherished piece of modern Jewish wisdom is to "Pray as if it is all up to God; act as if it is all up to you." Pray and hope, yes, but put feet under your prayers. I cannot help thinking about James Baldwin in Paris in 1963, standing up in the American Church on the Left Bank to enlist support for a march to the American Embassy. Of the pictures of Baldwin leading that march in Paris, and then flying to Washington, where, even though he was kept off the dais by those who thought he was too controversial, he listened to and publicly supported the speeches up to and including Dr. King's "I Have a Dream."

What is the New Jerusalem that Baldwin so often spoke about and said he was working toward? It is the fulfillment of God's promises for humanity. The melding of the temporal city of humans with the City of God about which Augustine of Hippo wrote so long ago. It is a place where, in the words of the prophet Amos, justice will roll like a river and righteousness like a mighty stream.[67] It is a future place where, as the prophet Isaiah said, the wolf will lie down with the lamb, and no harm or violence will be done on all of God's holy mountain.[68]

But that New Jerusalem does not come on its own.

It is not enough to be a witness, or simply to hope for it. You have to pray with your feet as well as your voice. To get people to march, to vote, and to seek change, they have to be convinced in their heads and hearts that this is their calling—and so, over and over again, across the decades, Baldwin recommitted himself to this work. In the process, he changed hearts and minds, including mine.

Toward the end of writing this book, I was made aware of an injustice at work in an institution I love. Even though this injustice seemed to be connected with real human suffering, it would have been easier to say nothing. To do nothing.

I found that I could not ignore Baldwin's example. I was called to be a witness, and not to speak out would be to side with injustice. Remember Baldwin's comments on the status quo: if things remain the way they are, then we remain in a state of injustice, because the status quo does not want to be changed.

I don't think of myself as a brave person, and with good reason. I was terrified that speaking out would have consequences. It did. Some people didn't like what I had pointed out, and they were cruel about their disagreement. I felt that the institution I love might think differently of me because I had called it to do better. I was rattled by the vast number of voices called into conversation, even though the great majority of them agreed with me. "It's always scary speaking up and out," my wife, Jeanie, texted, for like Baldwin, I was far from home when I did so, and it was uncomfortable.

But like so many of his readers over the years, I come back to Baldwin's core desire, expressed in *Notes from a Native Son*, to be an honest man and a truth-teller. If all of us who love and admire Baldwin take that calling seriously—to be honest about ourselves and about the world, to call out what is wrong, to stand up for what is right—then we have no choice but to speak, preach, teach, write, march, vote, transport, feed, house, nurture, boycott, and lend our feet and heads and hands to the quest for justice.

Only in these ways will we ever see more than the vague outlines of this New Jerusalem. Like Baldwin, I fear I may never set foot in it. But I would dearly love to be within sight of the city walls before I go.

Baldwin on Identity

"Be careful what you set your heart on,"
someone once said to me, "for it will surely be yours."
Well, I had said that I was going to be a writer,
God, Satan, and Mississippi notwithstanding,
and that color did not matter, and that I was going to be free.

—James Baldwin, *Nobody Knows My Name*

When you look at the range of titles of Baldwin's published works, it's somewhat startling to see how many of those titles seem to be about a lack of knowing or being known; about a sense of loss; about, as my student Daniel Smith noted, alienation from oneself or from others: *Another Country, Tell Me How Long the Train's Been Gone, Nobody Knows My Name, No Name in the Street.* Identity is a serious subject for James Baldwin, and it must be, Daniel suggested, for anyone reading him: "The ideal reader of Baldwin … if he wants to do real justice to Baldwin's outlook, he will need to do nothing less than rattle the foundations of his own ruins. He will of his own free will ask challenging questions about himself and his fellow man, about the evil of history, and some of this will be uncomfortable, and that's okay.... And if nothing else, the reader of Baldwin can almost certainly do no worse than evolve further into his truest self."[1]

In my early years teaching at Baylor, I had students tell me about a white male professor of religion who opened the first day of class by walking through an alphabet of identification. He told them all the things he was, because, he rightly believed, it made a difference not only in how he interpreted Scripture, but in how he saw the world: "I'm an American. A Baptist. A Christian. A Democrat. I'm evangelical." And so on and so on. I'd love to have known what he had for x and z, but to be sure, it was a full-fledged parade of identifications.

He knew who he was. And unlike Baldwin's book title, after that performance, everyone knew his name.

What we are—or what people think we are—is one of the most significant things that shapes us. It can weigh on us; it can liberate us; or it can simply be the constant filter through which we see the world. Baldwin's interviewers were often fascinated by the various ways he might be defined: American. Black. Expatriate. Gay. Male. And so on and so on. But he, we will see, resisted those attempts at definition—and while self-definition was certainly better than being defined by others, Baldwin wasn't sure that it was always good to define himself at all.

One day, he hoped, when we reach that New Jerusalem, when we all sit at the Welcome Table, there will be no need for names, labels, distinctions, or identities that divide or group us. Not the ones imposed on us by others, nor the ones we choose to use to define ourselves. Take, for example, the words we use to define those whose parents are of different races. In the bad old days, we had bad old names for them. Mulatto. Quadroon. Half-caste perhaps is marginally better, but still wrong. Offensive. Hateful even. Would we still say "mixed-race"?

And then the questions arise: Why do we have to call them anything at all? Why do we have to have a category for human beings, a convenient box in which to drop a human life?

Won't there come a day—in the New Jerusalem or when we gather at the Welcome Table—when we won't ask what someone is but simply see them as who they are, that is to say, just another human being?

It's a challenge because, as Baldwin notes, that's not the way we've done business up to now. Every one of us—white, Black, gay, straight, immigrant, homeschooled, private-schooled, Jewish, Sikh, Muslim, evangelical Baptist, conservative Catholic, liberal Episcopalian—defines ourselves or is defined in negative and positive ways.

When I tell nonreligious people, for example, that I am a Christian theologian, and their faces shrink with distaste before they can stop themselves, I have taken to instantly responding, "Oh, not that kind of Christian," because to be known, it feels like I must both point out what I am and what I am not. In this case, where people expect me to be a certain good or bad something based on how I am identified, there can be, as Baldwin notes, a painful collision between illusions and reality, myths and truth. I can avoid facing the truth about myself—or you can avoid seeing me as I truly am—by continuing to live inside an illusion provided by identity. It should not surprise us that Baldwin thinks we "will certainly perish" if we choose fantasy.[2]

In watching white and Black Americans encounter each other in Paris after World War II, Baldwin wrote that there was "the high potential of an awkward or an ugly situation" because of this phenomenon. When white Americans encounter Black Americans overseas, he noted, they do so "through a distorting screen created by a lifetime of conditioning. He is accustomed to regard him either as a needy and deserving martyr or as the soul of rhythm." Black Americans in Paris had found a home where they weren't purely defined by race, although this does not mean the French didn't have their own set of identifiers: "All Negroes arrive from America, trumpet-laden and twinkle-toed, bearing scars so unutterably painful that all of the glories of the French Republic may not suffice to heal them. This indignant generosity poses problems of its own."[3]

W. E. B. Du Bois famously wrote of a phenomenon he called "double-consciousness," the internal negotiations of this collision of identities for Black people as they encountered others who looked like themselves or others who didn't:

> The Negro is a sort of seventh son, born with a veil, and gifted with second-sight in this American world,—a world which yields him no self-consciousness, but only lets him see himself through the revelation of the other world. It is a peculiar sensation, this double-consciousness, this sense of always looking at one's self through the eyes of others, of measuring one's soul by the tape of a world that looks on in amused contempt and pity. One feels his two-ness,—an American, a Negro; two souls, two thoughts, two unreconciled strivings; two warring ideals in one dark body, whose dogged strength alone keeps it from being torn asunder. The history of the American Negro is the history of this strife.[4]

I suspect that some version of this double-consciousness operates in us when we aren't sure how our perceived and actual identities may need to be reconciled in public performance, in what we do and say and how we do those things. Am I gay enough in this space; am I too gay? Am I scholarly enough for this gathering of scholars? Am I angry enough to fit in at this protest rally?

Anthony Reddie has talked about what it's like to weigh every situation, every room he walks into to decide precisely what and who he should be, what he is able and unable to say based on how he is perceived. Baldwin spoke of this phenomenon more than once. A man who looks like him, he wrote in *Notes of a Native Son*, "has learned to anticipate: as the mouth opens, he divines what the tongue will utter."[5] And these interactions could change, modified, for example, by the type of person encountered.

Baldwin had been defined by others from an early age. White America had decided who and what he was before it even knew him, before he had even drawn breath. Late in life, he told an interviewer that what he got from France was what he could not get in America: "a sense of 'If I can do it, I may do it.' I won't generalize, but in the years I grew up in the U.S., I could not do that. I'd already been defined."[6] This is one of the crowning harms of racism: that it defines others, often to their detriment, or it reduces the beauties and rhythms of their lives and cultures into something to be regarded with shame.

Baldwin told Studs Terkel that he had to relearn pride in himself and in his heritage to be able to write a successful novel about Harlem. That first winter in Switzerland with his lover Lucien Happersberger in the family chalet, Baldwin realized what had kept him from finishing *Go Tell It on the Mountain*: "I was ashamed of where I came from and where I had been. I was ashamed of the life in the Negro church, ashamed of my father, ashamed of the Blues, ashamed of Jazz, and of course ashamed of watermelon: all of those stereotypes that the country inflicts on Negroes. . . . Well, I was afraid of all that: and I ran from it."

Studs Terkel asked, "Did you feel a sense of shame about a heritage that is really so *rich*, when you accepted the white man's stereotype of yourself?"

Baldwin replied that of course he did, that this was one of the great hazards of being Black in America. He said, "All you are ever told in this country about being black is that it is a terrible, terrible thing to be." And to survive this, "You have to *decide* who you are, and force the world to deal with you, not with its *idea* of you."[7]

Baldwin had written in "Stranger in the Village" about the experience of being an exotic creature in Leukerbad/Loèche-les-Bains, of being followed and shouted at by children who had never seen a Black person. It was in Switzerland that he not only recovered his awareness and pride in his identity and culture, but came to essential understandings about the collision of Black and white identities—that he could accept his past, and as he listened to the blues of Bessie Smith, recalled and recast the shouting of the Black church, the language of his childhood, and the identity that was beautifully his, not the one imposed upon him. As he told Terkel, he had to relearn what being Black meant: "I couldn't accept what I had been told."[8]

Baldwin's books, his narratives and essays, are full of examples of those who have accepted their identity based on what others told them. In *The Fire Next Time*, Baldwin tells his nephew that Baldwin's own father "had a terrible life; he was defeated long before he died because, at the bottom of his heart, he really believed what white people said about him."[9] In *One Day When I Was Lost*, young Malcolm Little tells a favorite white teacher about his dream of practicing law. He asks about schools, how best to proceed, and the teacher, Mr. Ostrovski, encourages him to accept a different sort of identification: "I don't want you to be hurt—that's the important thing—the important thing about a life is to be realistic, Malcolm. Colored people can't become lawyers. You know that. So, you have to decide to do something a colored person can do."[10]

The same kind of identities are enforced on white people, also to their detriment. As a youngster, I was told that white people didn't like soul music. White people didn't dance (if they had just told me, "You don't dance well," that would have been purest truth). They didn't associate with people of other races. All of those notions limited us as well as being potentially harmful to others. In *Blues for Mister Charlie*, one of the most poignant lines comes from Lyle as he speaks to Parnell, the white newspaper owner who has tried to walk back and forth between the Black and white communities: "What's the matter with you? Have you forgotten you a white man?"[11] The identity and the roles it imposes upon him are why, Lyle confesses, he killed young Richard. He had to, because of this imposed identity. "I had to kill him then! I'm a white man! Can't nobody talk that way to *me*!"[12]

Identity is an alphabet soup, and I hope as you read about these white and Black identities, you'll recognize that all of us have had identifications people have wanted to force upon us, mythologies they would use to limit our human capability. In *The Evidence of Things Not Seen*, for example, Baldwin not only spoke of how European immigrants to America were forced to put on a white mainstream American identity—to become white—if they wanted to survive and thrive; he also writes of gender roles, how men identify with a set of qualities and realities that they often can't live up to. To be a man humiliated, Baldwin writes, "obliterates him." If he finds he can't take care of his family, "he finds it, literally, impossible to face them." Women, for their part, manage somehow "to survive and surmount being defined by others. They dismiss the definition, however dangerous or wounding it may be—or even, sometimes, find a way to utilize it."[13] The act of external definition may indeed be wounding to all of us so defined, but if it can be set aside, if "you have to *decide* who you are, and force the world to deal with you, not with its *idea* of you," then this shaming can be, as Baldwin discovered in Switzerland and over the rest of his life, a tool that allows you to define yourself on your own terms.

Even if you recognize, as Baldwin and the future Malcolm X and Parnell do, that these enforced identities don't encompass who you are, they still have power and can be dangerous or wounding. When asked about what he thinks of criticism, Baldwin replied, "It is never entirely true that you don't give a shit what others say about you, but you must throw it out of your mind. I went through a very trying period, after all, where on one side of town I was an Uncle Tom and on the other the Angry Young Man. It could make one's head spin, the number of labels that have been attached to me. And it was inevitably painful, and surprising, and bewildering."[14]

And what people think about us—the myths they've embraced, the identities that they imagine we inhabit—have broken us individually and communally. Baldwin often wrote about how the ideas white people had about Black people were partly so that the former could divine where they stood in the cosmic scheme—and how they allowed them not to wonder too deeply about Black people and their plight. Speaking in the South to a white principal whose high school was being integrated by fits and starts, Baldwin listened to him talk about the mixing of the races, and then claim that he had never held ill will toward any "colored person." Baldwin believed him, he says. "But I could not avoid wondering if he had ever really looked at a Negro and wondered about the life, the aspirations, the universal humanity hidden behind the dark skin."[15]

In Baldwin's imaginative literature, "blackness" and "whiteness" are often set off from each other as simultaneous acts of definition. Black people are told what they are by whites, and white people accept their own definitions and define themselves in response to them. What happens to Black characters in *Tell Me How Long the Train's Been Gone*, or *Another Country*, or *Go Tell It on the Mountain* are many times a direct result of these imposed definitions and counterdefinitions. They also deeply complicate relationships between white and Black characters, since the white characters are equally mired in the definitions their culture has tried to impose on them. In *Another Country*, Vivaldo's relationship with Ida is strained by each of their attempts to navigate racial definitions; Cass's friendship with Ida runs headlong into Ida's experiences of being defined as Black; even Rufus's experience of being chewed up by the city is partly explained by how Rufus is seen and sees himself. Baldwin said, in agreeing with an interviewer, that in that novel, how characters were defined racially in the United States (the "country" of the title) was essential to the story itself.[16]

Worse still is when people try to become something they are not in order to live up to normative definitions, standards that insist, for example, that one is somehow lesser if not straight, white, and Christian (and male, if at all possible). This "American image" that Baldwin writes about unites (or purports to unite) all Americans around the set of shared values promoted by the ruling classes: hard work, chastity, piety, success. Such definitions of what it means to be a true American, as Baldwin notes, leave out "most of the people in the country, and most of the facts of life."[17] People look at themselves in the mirror, or look down at their lives, and they cannot help but be failures in comparison. As Baldwin said, he looked up at one point and realized that he was not now and never would be white, and in

"The Harlem Ghetto" he writes, "It seems to me quite logical that any minority identified by the color of its skin and the texture of its hair would eventually grow self-conscious about these attributes."[18]

One can despair of these definitions, these standards. Or one can decide to reject them and create more truthful ones, more liberating ones.

Baldwin said that one can realize that how others define you does not have to be how you define yourself: "Perhaps the turning point in one's life is realizing that to be treated like a victim is not necessarily to become one."[19] It puts me in mind of a stirring scene from Spike Lee's *BlacKkKlansman* (even more powerful in the screenplay) as activist Kwame Ture talks with an audience of Black college students in mostly white Colorado Springs, Colorado, about how they should react to societal definitions. Ture says, "Is Beauty defined by someone with a Narrow Nose? Thin Lips? White Skin? You ain't got none of that.... We want to be like the White people that oppress us in this Country and since they hate us, we hate ourselves."[20]

Baldwin uses scenes from Malcolm X's life in *One Day When I Was Lost* to explore white definitions of beauty. Malcolm Little painfully straightens his kinky hair with lye into a "conk." Malcolm later said of himself and others who pursued this fashion that it "makes you wonder if the Negro has completely lost all sense of identity, lost touch with himself."[21] In one of the most poignant moments in *One Day When I Was Lost*, Baldwin identifies Malcolm's movement toward the Nation of Islam, when his prison mentor Luther challenges him:

> You don't want to look like what you are. What makes you ashamed of what you are? ... The white man sees you and he laughs. He *laughs*. Because he knows you ain't

white. But as long as you want to be white, he's got you where he wants you.[22]

When myths and stereotypes and arbitrary standards impose identities on any of us, it's essential that we come back to Baldwin's revelation that we are allowed to decide for ourselves who we are, how we understand and value ourselves. That Bessie Smith and jazz are gifts to the universe. Or that our looks and our lives are truly beautiful. In *BlacKkKlansman*, Kwame Ture's speech powerfully expresses a people's choice to define themselves, and more importantly, to love themselves.

Though it takes time and effort, Black people can throw off the lies and "their Shaming effect on Black Minds," and Black people can accept themselves and love themselves without reference to artificial imposed standards:

> *Your Nose is Boss, your Lips are*
> *Thick, your skin is Black, you are*
> *Black and you are Beautiful!*[23]

"To be liberated from the stigma of blackness by embracing it," Baldwin says, "is to cease, forever, one's interior agreement and collaboration with the authors of one's degradation."[24]

Black people should get to decide for themselves what beauty is. Gay and trans people should be able to judge for themselves how their lives are in search of the love and passion we all desire and seek. Religious people, if they are living out the core teachings of their traditions toward compassion and against domination, should be able to set their own definitions of what faithful practice means. And straight white Christian Americans, as they look at others, should be able to define themselves not purely in opposition to their gay siblings or their Black siblings or their non-Christian or immigrant siblings, but see themselves for themselves as well. "The black man has functioned in the white man's world," Baldwin says, "as an immovable pillar: and as he moves out of his place, heaven and earth are shaken to their foundations."[25] More powerfully, he told Kenneth Clark on television just after that failed meeting with Robert F. Kennedy, "What white people have to do, is to try to find out in their own hearts why it was necessary to have a nigger in the first place."[26]

May it be so. As we see all the harm done across the centuries by trying to impose definitions onto others—or even simply by our own failures to look closely enough to see honestly the definitions that shape our own lives—it becomes clear that Baldwin's call to self-definition is an essential step away from that harmful imposition of identity, that as Luther tells Malcolm when he agrees not to straighten his hair, maybe some people are too far gone. "But I got a message for you.... I can show you how to get out of prison."[27]

"It has always been much easier," Baldwin wrote in *Nothing Personal*, "to give a name to the evil without than to locate the terror within.... This terror has something to do with that irreducible gap between the self one invents—the self one takes oneself as being, which is, however, and by definition, a provisional self—and the undiscoverable self which always has the power to blow the provisional self to bits." In our lives, he said, we sometimes wake up, or pass through a door, and realize that "the self one has sewn together with such effort is all dirty rags, is unusable, is gone."[28]

For all of us—although perhaps especially those of us with privilege—this step into a new identity can be terrifying. But for all of us, it can be liberating, beautiful. And it is absolutely necessary.

Baldwin told Studs Terkel that, painful as it had sometimes been, he had to define himself. First, he said, as a writer. "I don't think … anybody in his right mind," he said, "would want to be a writer. But you do discover that you are a writer, and then you haven't got any choice. You live that life or you won't live any."[29] So, setting aside superficial questions of gender, sexuality, and race, Baldwin leaned into this understanding of himself based on who he was and what he did: *I'm a writer, an American writer, and wherever I am and whatever I do, my self-definition must grow out of this space.*

In thinking about oneself as an American, Baldwin noted, one might choose from a multitude of identities, despite the homogeneous white male Christian version mostly on offer. "Which America will you have?" he asked. All of the various "Americas," he said, "diverge significantly and sometimes dangerously."[30]

As Baldwin speaks in "The New Lost Generation" of people of his acquaintance, "some ceased fleeing and turned to face the demons that had been on the trail so long. The luckiest among us were these last, for they managed to go to pieces and then put themselves back together.… This may take away one's dreams, but it delivers one to oneself."[31] Whether that is national identity or sexual identity or what have you, to define oneself is gift.

In *Another Country*, Baldwin wrote about a liberating moment in the life of the Black female character Ida where she stepped up on stage and let her true self be heard:

> What she lacked in vocal power and, at the moment, in skill, she compensated for by a quality so mysteriously and implacably egocentric that no one has ever been able to name it. The quality involves a sense of the self so profound and so powerful that it does not so much leap barriers as reduce them to atoms—while still leaving them

standing, mightily, where they were; and this awful sense is private, unknowable, not to be articulated, having, literally, to do with something else; it transforms and lays waste and gives life, and kills.[32]

He noted that you could not shut out the knowledge of things that had been done to one because others had defined you in a negative fashion. But you could understand them in that way. You could develop your own profound sense of self and worth that would resist any outside attempt to define you narrowly or devalue you based on surface characteristics. Ida struggles throughout the book—as do other characters—with surface judgments made about color or gender or sexuality or artistic merit. She and Vivaldo fight often about the ways they misunderstand each other because of their lived identities. But they also strive to love hard across those boundaries, to live into that love that Baldwin placed as humanity's highest good—and that thing that helps us figure out who we are in all our beautiful complication.

In *The Amen Corner*, the dying father, Luke, tells his son David, "The most terrible time in a man's life . . . is when he's done lost everything that held him together." But, Luke advises, it doesn't take much to hold a person together. A human being can handle losing almost everything, "can even die with his head up . . . as long as he got that one thing. That one thing is *him*, David, who he is inside—and son, I don't believe no man ever got to that without somebody loved him."[33]

Baldwin resisted categories to the extent that it became clear that what he hoped for was that at some point—in some future New Jerusalem, at some Welcome Table—we would lay down our definitions and labels just as the spiritual "Down by the Riverside" says we will someday lay down our sword and shield.

At last, perhaps we return to Baldwin the artist and critic for help, to the writer who understands that to insist on labeling our complex humanity is to reduce us to one-dimensional stereotypes. It is impossible, Baldwin insists

> to write a worthwhile novel about a Jew or a Gentile or a Homosexual, for people refuse, unhappily, to function in so neat and one-dimensional a fashion.... A novel insistently demands the presence and passion of human beings, who cannot ever be labeled. Once the novelist has created a human being he has shattered the label and, in transcending the subject matter, is able, for the first time, to tell us something about it and to reveal how profoundly all things involving human beings interlock.[34]

"Your people are all people," Baldwin told Jordan Elgrably toward the end of their long "Art of Fiction" interview for *Paris Review*.[35] It was that simple; nothing more and nothing less. Elgrably himself read *Giovanni's Room* as "an attempt to break down these divisions, pointing out that David could be white, black, or yellow" (and, presumably, gay or straight; male, female, or other). Baldwin agreed. "In terms of what happened to him," he said, "none of that mattered at all."[36] The story is not about whom he loves or how he loves. Baldwin always insisted that although the book was claimed by and a comfort to the gay community, *Giovanni's Room* was not really about homosexuality but about the universal question of loving and not loving enough, "of what happens to you if you're afraid to love somebody."[37]

Love is love, Baldwin said in his writing and in interviews. To limit it, or to insist on channeling it, is wrong and perhaps even immoral. Perhaps this was why, just as Baldwin wanted

Americans to find an identity and equity that transcended race, he also responded to questions about his sexuality by resisting definitions beyond the act of loving. In an interview with the *Village Voice*, Baldwin said that the word "gay" had never resonated with him, that how he loved and who he loved was "absolutely personal. It was really a matter between me and God. I would have to live the life he had made me to live." That universal question of loving and not loving enough has nothing to do with what you call that love. "Loving anybody and being loved by anybody," he argued, "is a tremendous danger, a tremendous responsibility."[38]

That question, danger, and responsibility are taken up in many of Baldwin's creative works. Baldwin leans into it theologically in *The Amen Corner*, when Sister Boxer takes her pastor, Sister Margaret, to task for her lack of compassion for her dying former husband: "The Word do say, if you can't love your brother who you can see, how you going to love God, who you ain't seen?"[39]

Vivaldo, in *Another Country*, wonders if he had loved Rufus fearlessly enough, if he might have helped his friend find enough hope and courage to stay alive: "I wondered, I guess I still wonder, what would have happened if I'd taken him in my arms, if I'd held him, if I hadn't been—afraid. I was afraid that he wouldn't understand that it was—only love. Only love. But, oh, Lord, when he died, I thought that maybe I could have saved him if I'd just reached out the quarter of an inch between us on that bed, and held him."[40]

In *If Beale Street Could Talk*, Tish's father, Joseph, observes as Fonny's father, Frank, angrily tells his estranged daughters to go to bed, to get out of his sight, and realizes that they do love each other but somehow cannot communicate it: "He sees something strange, something he had never thought of: he sees that Adrienne loves her father with a really desperate love. She knows he is in pain. She would soothe it if she could, she does not know how. She would give anything to know how."[41] Frank, like Rufus, does not survive the story in which he is a character. One has to wonder, and I'm sure Baldwin is asking, if Frank had known that powerful sense of love from his daughters—from his wife—might he have lived long enough to see his son released from jail?

Hall Montana, brother of the dead Arthur in Baldwin's last novel, *Just above My Head*, is stricken by the failure to love after he receives the news of this brother's death: "Do you know, do you know how much my brother loved me? how much he loved me? And do you know I did not know it? did not dare to know it: do *you* know? No. No. No."[42] He rails against himself for that divide, now that it cannot be repaired.

In most of Baldwin's work, in fact, these failures to love sacrificially, failures to love with courage, failures to love in the face of whatever others might say about that love, doom characters. Even in *The Welcome Table*, where Baldwin was wrestling with his late-life inclinations about the necessity of love and the irrelevance of labels, we find characters trying to live into the importance of love. Rob says to his lover, Mark, that no matter how many women he's been with—or how many children he might have—these things do not and cannot define him. Whatever the circumstances of my life, Rob tells Mark, he will always love him. That when he's old and dying, it will be Mark to whom his thoughts turn.[43]

Thankfully we have found powerful exceptions in his work to what Baldwin presents as this great sin, people who are not lost but who reach across barriers and love freely. *Beale Street* is full of sacrificial love that vaults across categories. When Fonny's and Tish's families find out that the unmarried Tish is carrying

Fonny's baby, Fonny's very religious mother and sisters call Tish a sinner. Mrs. Hunt says Tish has a demon, that she is trying to destroy her son, and tells the room that she hopes the Holy Ghost will shrivel up that child of sin in Tish's womb.

Tish's mother, father, and older sister earlier had responded to the news not by shaming Tish but with resolute and unconditional love. This will not be a child of sin, a bastard, or any category of name one might attach to a human being; this child simply will be beautiful, welcomed, and loved. Her mother brings out that very old bottle of French brandy they've been saving for a special occasion. Her father pours. They raise their glasses. "This is sacrament," Tish's mother says. And later, Tish sits on her father's lap; he kisses her on the forehead and runs his hand through her hair. "You're a good girl, Clementine," he tells her. "I'm proud of you. Don't you forget that."[44]

It is indeed, as Tish says, a miracle to realize that you are loved.

Another powerful exception to the lost and isolated condition of humankind can be seen in the journey of Malcolm X in *One Day When I Was Lost*. Had he not gone on the pilgrimage to Mecca, perhaps Malcolm too would have gone the way of characters like David in *Giovanni's Room*, afraid to love, trapped in categories and in self-loathing. After he returns, Malcolm's love for his family and for all humankind is liberating, even though he does not survive to fully live into that love. Near the end of the screenplay, we see that Malcolm has changed from a young man riddled with hatred to a man filled with love.

In Baldwin's final work, *The Welcome Table*, we see an extension of this love across boundaries, across race and faith and gender and any sort of identity. If we were describing these characters by the categories in which they fit, we'd say they include an elderly white Frenchwoman whose family lost their land and wealth when they were forced to leave Algeria; a native

Algerian, who should be counterposed to her; Christian and Jew, male and female, Black and white, wealthy and poor. In Baldwin's notes on casting, he indicates that several of the characters would be identified as white, or pass as white—it's almost as though he doesn't want to impose that description of color upon them. And while several of the characters are not conventionally heterosexual, he doesn't seek to define them in that way. Baldwin, who spoke of our commonality, said, "There's nothing in me that is not in everybody else, and nothing in everybody else that is not in me."[45]

Throughout the drafts of the play, the same theme, centered around the title, emerges: who we are, where we come from, how others identify us, how we love, whom we love—all those boxes people use to sort us and keep us—don't ultimately matter in the least. In the world to come—at the Welcome Table—we'll simply be human, exulting in our connections, not seeking ways to distinguish ourselves from each other. When James Baldwin said he was walking toward the New Jerusalem, he said it would be a world where "No one will have to call themselves gay," and in that time and place, "there will no longer be anything to prove. The world will belong to all of us."[46]

An essential job of any writer, Baldwin says, is to unite things, "to find the terms of our connection, without which we will perish."[47] Bad art leaves us locked into our separate rooms, does not tell us the truth about who we are individually and communally, imagines that we can define each other or that we require definition.

And where Baldwin leaves us on this question is on the journey he urged us to take: to reject the status quo, to wrestle with our own sense of importance and awareness of worth, and to work toward a future where hatred and prejudice will, always, be overwhelmed by love.

Journey's End, New Beginnings

There is never time in the future in which
we will work out our salvation.
The challenge is in the moment, the time is always now.

—James Baldwin, *No Name in the Street*

In the summer of 2022, as I was nearing the end of my years working on this book, I left the American Cathedral in Paris in the early morning and spent a long summer day traveling back to Leukerbad, Switzerland. I made the long, winding bus journey back up into the Alps, my eyes resolutely focused on my copy of *No Name in the Streets*. I took an apartment a couple hundred yards from where James Baldwin and Lucien Happersberger stayed on those occasions that were so central to Baldwin's life, work, and thought.

While there, I set down this book you have been reading to do the final edit of a novel I had spent six years writing. I thought that one of the ways I could best connect with Baldwin in Switzerland was to follow again in his footsteps, to do the work he had done so well when he finished *Go Tell It on the Mountain* after many years and many iterations.

I moved a table out onto my patio and set up my computer there. My view as I worked was the view that Baldwin had from the Happersberger chalet. Across the valley, a waterfall or three dropped off the Alps. The prospect was dominated by the ninety-six-hundred-foot-tall Daubenhorn, which I understand has a Swiss-engineered set of ladders, cables, and cable bridges an expert climber can take up to the top. I hiked the paths, but I no more considered that climb than Baldwin might have.

I had decided back before the pandemic that I wanted to go on a journey with Baldwin and see where it led me. In addition to teaching his work in formal and informal settings, I wanted to challenge myself with rarely considered Baldwin writings. I wanted to listen to his voice and watch him on film. To sit in cafés in Paris and soul-food joints in Harlem, and to roam the American South that had taken all of Baldwin's courage to visit. To read letters to and from him, about him, that have never been published. To touch manuscripts he had written, read his longhand corrections, learn about the work he was hoping to complete before he died.

But like every journey—like the one you and I have taken together in this book—the physical and exterior details are only a tiny part of the work. In reading and rereading Baldwin, in confronting the full scope of his life and experience, I felt that I was learning from him not just about the larger themes we've explored but about every part of the human experience. In writing this book, I felt that I was being challenged, as Baldwin put it, to do better. To love my wife and family more fiercely. To cling to some kind of faith more powerfully. To reach out across the divides of race and culture. To be a witness to injustice, even when it cost me something.

At the conclusion of this work, I remain what I was at the beginning: a straight white Christian American male. All those qualifiers still mark me and might conceivably separate me from people I have grown to love, people whose qualifiers are markedly different from mine and perhaps even at cross-purposes to them.

But I feel differently, not that Baldwin and I ever had serious disagreements before I was inspired to write about him. I feel like all of those things I said I felt about Baldwin in the introduction are truer now than they were before.

That as a writer, a teacher, a preacher, a lover, and a fighter, Baldwin has both inspired me to do more and taught me how to do better.

That as I sat revising my novel, I could feel Baldwin's influence on my characters, my style, and my view of the world.

I am still me. But as with every great teacher, as with every encounter with great art, Baldwin has left me as more me than I ever was. In a good way.

This book is not about—and was never meant to be about—its author. When my story has squeaked into these pages, I've tried to use it as a way to point back to James Baldwin, to help illuminate his story and his stories. But throughout, we've also witnessed other readers, lovers, believers, and artists whose stories have been shaped by their encounters with Baldwin, and I suspect that you have been and will be one of those folks as well.

When I wrote early on that every age is an age of Baldwin, what I think I meant—and now I'm sure I mean—is that we need him to teach us that however difficult the present moment, we can respond to it with courage and can demand the truth. That in place of hatred and division, we can understand each other better, love each other more. That each of us has infinite worth, each of us is created in beauty.

That in the final analysis, there is hope.

I have needed these messages across the past few years, as perhaps you have. And I know I will need them again. Baldwin calls us to many things, but ultimately what I think I know best after this long journey—what I know I was feeling as I finished my novel in the Switzerland village where Baldwin used to roam—is that life is beautiful and it is meant to be lived, and we all have to have the courage to live it.

Baldwin said that you have to go the way your blood beats. "If you don't live the only life you have," he said, "you won't live some other life, you won't live any life at all. That's the only advice you can give anybody."[1]

What this journey with Baldwin has inspired me to do is live the only life I have. To climb the Alps—metaphorically at least—and not settle for a safe life on the plains. To find out what I think and what I have to say. To think about what it means to be a witness to another's suffering or another's triumph.

At the end of this process, I don't have the sense that Baldwin was any more flawless than I am. Far from it. But in his flaws, his fears, his failures, I find this real person who loved and was loved, who made art and influenced art, who saw injustice and spoke out against injustice, and who continues to speak truth into this age and into the age to come.

I saw a person who struggled day to day, yet could ask his family or his friends to pray that he might write well and act rightly.

That's me. And most of those whose voices appear in this text. And probably you.

Saints are not saints because they're picture-perfect. They're saints because they show up and put their hands in the real and get them dirty. And they're saints because they inspire us.

So, to Blessed St. James of Harlem and Paris and Saint-Paul-de-Vence: Thank you, dear friend, for your life. Thank you for your work. It meant something, it means something, and it will always mean something.

Sister Margaret in *The Amen Corner* illuminates the meaning of the closing word "Amen." It means "Let it be so."[2]

So we've learned that Baldwin believed that two truths summed up his total knowledge about the world.

> *Live the life you're given.*
> *We can be better.*
> *And I can only say, Amen.*
> *May it be so.*

Acknowledgments

Just to be clear, this was not my great idea. Two publishing professionals planted the idea of this book a number of years ago. Carey Newman, then at the Baylor University Press, and Lara Heimert of Basic Books suggested that a book about the wisdom of James Baldwin would be a strong book that I could write well. My agent and friend Andrea Heinecke at the Bindery Agency encouraged and helped me shape the proposal for this book, and Jon Sweeney at Orbis Books brought an enthusiasm for the project and an expertise I've relied on in our past work together. I hope this book lives up to their vision for it.

In the research and writing, I've been bulwarked by incredible institutional and financial resources. Baylor University, my teaching home for over thirty years, offered me the chance to introduce Baldwin to students in film, literature, and race and culture classes, and in the fall of 2022 released me from teaching to work full-time on this book and on projects on race and reconciliation. I am grateful to Lee Nordt, dean of the College of Arts and Sciences; to Kevin Gardner, my department chair; and to all my Baylor colleagues who worked around my absence and encouraged this labor. I also owe a huge debt to Dean Todd Still of Baylor's Truett Theological Seminary for the use of Truett's lodgings at the University of Oxford where I read and wrote, as well as for our work together on many of the issues of race and religion explored herein.

The Baugh Family Foundation and James and Lydia Perry provided external funding for this and related work, and made possible research, collaboration, and writing across the United States and overseas. Without their generosity this book could not have been completed so well or so quickly—or perhaps at all. I am grateful to Regents Park College at the University of Oxford and to the Oxford Centre for Faith and Culture for the opportunity to speak to scholars and students, and for a fall 2021 fellowship at the centre. Professor Anthony Reddie, who ably heads the centre, encouraged this work, and our shared passion for Baldwin and our friendship was a great gift to me.

I was greeted upon productive writing retreats in 2021 and 2022 at Gladstone's Library in Hawarden, Wales, by past warden Peter Francis and present warden Andrea Russell, and by the always-helpful staff. Bob and Sheryl Cox invited me to write at their Colorado cabin on several occasions, which helped me stay on schedule on this and other projects, and helped keep me sane. I seem to breathe easier in the mountains. Alison Nathan likewise welcomed me to use her lake house in Kingsland, Texas, where I have been grateful to write since her father, Terry, of Blessed Memory, first invited me there in 2012. These gifts of time, space, and focus have been invaluable, and I am so very thankful.

In the summer of 2022 Reggie Williams talked with me about Baldwin's connections with the American Church in Paris, where Reggie was serving as visiting theologian. Reggie's American Church lectures on Black Paris and Monique Wells's walking tour of Black Paris gave me new insights about Baldwin and the world he inhabited, including the location of Chez Inez, the jazz club where Baldwin literally sang for his supper. I relied on the American Library in Paris, where I am a proud member, for borrowing privileges and writing space over numerous trips. Finally, I am completing this draft—and typing these very words—on a cold, dark night in the tower apartment of the American Cathedral of the Holy Trinity in Paris, France. I have been honored to serve, first as Theologian in Residence and, since 2021, as Canon Theologian of the cathedral, and have been and will always be grateful for support from Past Dean Lucinda Laird, Interim Dean Tim Safford, our amazing staff, and the congregation of this great institution.

I am so grateful for the life, work, and legacy of James Baldwin. I've sought to use his own brilliant words as often as possible to support my arguments, while remaining mindful of the principle of fair use that limits quotation of other writers. I've also sought to be respectful of the rights of the Baldwin family in my references to the James Baldwin collection at the Schomburg Research Center for Black Culture in Harlem, and have made sure not to employ any matter there that has not previously been published.

My greatest debt, as ever, is to my own family. My wife, Jeanie, has made incredible sacrifices so that I could travel and do this work, as have our daughters, Lily and Sophia. I apologize for every school pickup I missed and sleepover I didn't monitor, but I swear on St. James, I will make it up to all of you. I am most thankful to Jeanie, to the girls, and to my boys, Jake and Chandler, because they have taught me that what James Baldwin says about the power and primacy of love is absolutely true.

I am a witness.

Notes

On Pilgrimage, Seeking St. James

1   Nicholas Buccola, "Five Things I've Learned about Freedom from Frederick Douglass," Myfivethings.com.
2   Daniel Smith, "Sketches on James Baldwin," email to author, July 5, 2022.
3   Ella Prichard, "James Baldwin," email to author, October 20, 2022.
4   Michael Eric Dyson, *What Truth Sounds Like: Robert F. Kennedy, James Baldwin, and Our Unfinished Conversation about Race in America* (New York: St. Martin's Press, 2018), 5–6.
5   "Movements for Change: The Bob Fitch Photography Archive at Stanford Libraries," Stanford Libraries.
6   Suzy Hansen, "Unlearning the Myth of American Innocence," *The Guardian*, August 8, 2017.
7   Robert P. Jones, "Gratitude for the Incandescent Witness of James Baldwin," September 24, 2021, *White Too Long*, Substack.
8   Maya Angelou, "A Brother's Love," in *James Baldwin: The Legacy*, ed. Quincy Troupe (New York: Touchstone, 1989), 42.
9   Baldwin, "The Price of the Ticket," in *James Baldwin: Collected Essays*, ed. Toni Morrison (New York: Library of America, 1998), 841.

The Life of James Baldwin

1   Baldwin, from *Notes of a Native Son*, in *James Baldwin: Collected Essays*, 63.
2   Susan McWilliams, "On the Faiths of (and in) Our Fathers," Frederick Douglass Forum, Linfield College, May 8, 2015; Nicholas Buccola, email to author, November 30, 2019.
3   Baldwin, *Notes of a Native Son*, 65.

4   Raoul Peck and James Baldwin, *I Am Not Your Negro* (New York: Vintage, 2017), 19.
5   Ibid.
6   Baldwin, from *The Fire Next Time*, in *James Baldwin: Collected Essays*, 308.
7   Baldwin, from *The Devil Finds Work*, in *James Baldwin: Collected Essays*, 502–3.
8   Nicholas Buccola, *The Fire Is upon Us: James Baldwin, William F. Buckley Jr., and the Debate over Race in America* (Princeton, NJ: Princeton University Press, 2019), 40.
9   James Campbell, *Exiled in Paris: Richard Wright, James Baldwin, Samuel Beckett, and Others on the Left Bank* (Berkeley: University of California Press, 2003), 9.
10   Richard Goldstein, "'Go the Way Your Blood Beats': An Interview with James Baldwin," in *James Baldwin: The Legacy*, 176.
11   Baldwin, from *No Name in the Street*, in *James Baldwin: Collected Essays*, 432.
12   Susan J. McWilliams, "Introduction," in *A Political Companion to James Baldwin*, ed. Susan J. McWilliams (Lexington: University Press of Kentucky, 2017), *passim*.

Baldwin as Prophet of Humanity

1   Jill Lepore, *These Truths: A History of the United States* (New York: Norton, 2018), xix–xx; Peck and Baldwin, *I Am Not Your Negro*, 107.
2   Peck and Baldwin, *I Am Not Your Negro*, 86.
3   Gwendolyn Brooks, "James Baldwin Reading from His Works," Library of Congress, Washington, DC, April 28, 1986.
4   Baldwin, "The American Dream and the American Negro," *New York Times*, March 7, 1965.
5   Jeremiah 7:1–7 NRSV.
6   Wen Stephenson, "American Jeremiad: A Manifesto," *New York Times*, March 23, 2010.
7   Baldwin, "Autobiographical Notes," in *James Baldwin: Collected Essays*, 9.
8   Baldwin, *No Name in the Street,* 432.
9   "William Faulkner Banquet Speech," nobelprize.org.
10   Sharifa Rhodes-Pitts, *Harlem Is Nowhere: A Journey to the Mecca of Black America* (New York: Little, Brown and Co., 2011), 107.

Baldwin on Culture

1   Baldwin, from *The Devil Finds Work*, 571.
2   Baldwin, "On the Painter Beauford Delaney," in *James Baldwin: Collected Essays*, 720.
3   Noah Berlatsky, "The Most Powerful Piece of Film Criticism Ever Written," *The Atlantic*, April 22, 2014.
4   Walker Percy, "The Diagnostic Novel: On the Uses of Modern Fiction," *The Atlantic*, June 1986.
5   Baldwin, "The Creative Process," in *James Baldwin: Collected Essays*, 669.
6   Baldwin, *Giovanni's Room* (New York: Vintage, 2013), 5; Baldwin, *The Devil Finds Work,* 571.
7   Buccola, *The Fire Is upon Us*, 3.
8   Baldwin, "Autobiographical Notes," 8.
9   Baldwin, "The Creative Process," 670.
10 Baldwin, "This Nettle, Danger . . . ," in *James Baldwin: Collected Essays*, 687.
11 Baldwin, "Words of a Native Son," in *James Baldwin: Collected Essays*, 708.
12 Douglas Field, "James Baldwin and the Art of Reviewing," *Small Axe*, December 2011.
13 Hilton Als, "The Enemy Within: The Making and Unmaking of James Baldwin," *The New Yorker*, February 9, 1998.
14 Jordan Elgrably, "James Baldwin, The Art of Fiction No. 78," *Paris Review* 91 (1984).
15 Mark Twain, "Fenimore Cooper's Literary Offenses," 1895.
16 Sydney Krause, *Mark Twain as Critic* (Baltimore: Johns Hopkins University Press, 2019).
17 Als, "The Enemy Within."
18 Baldwin, *Notes of a Native Son*, 11–12.
19 Ibid., 13.
20 Eldridge Cleaver, *Soul on Ice* (New York: Delta, 1968), 106.
21 Baldwin, "Alas Poor Richard," in *James Baldwin: Collected Essays*, 257.
22 Kichung Kim, "Wright, the Protest Novel, and Baldwin's Faith," *CLA Journal* 17, no. 3 (March 1974): 388.
23 Walt Whitman, "Song of Myself," 51, 1855/1892, Poets.org.
24 Baldwin, "Everybody's Protest Novel," 15–16.
25 Baldwin, *The Devil Finds Work*, 530.
26 Ibid., 533.
27 Julius Lester, "Reflections of a Maverick," *New York Times*, May 27, 1984.

28   Harriet Beecher Stowe, *Uncle Tom's Cabin: Or, Life among the Lowly*, ed. Christopher G. Diller (Peterborough, ON: Broadview, 2009), 455.

29   Baldwin, *If Beale Street Could Talk* (New York: Vintage, 2002), 4.

30   Ibid., 7.

31   Baldwin, *The Fire Next Time*, 293.

32   Ayana Mathis and Pankaj Mishra, "James Baldwin Denounced Richard Wright's 'Native Son' as a 'Protest Novel.' Was He Right?" *New York Times,* February 24, 2015.

33   Baldwin, "Everybody's Protest Novel," 12.

34   Robert Park Mills Papers, Box 2, Manuscript Collection MS-04872, Harry Ransom Center, University of Texas at Austin.

35   Baldwin, "The New Lost Generation," in *James Baldwin: Collected Essays*, 667.

36   Ibid., 668.

37   Anthony Reddie, "Dealing with the Two Deadly Ds: Deconstructing Whiteness and Decolonising the Curriculum," David Nicholls Memorial Lecture, Regent's Park College, Oxford, England, November 10, 2021.

38   Greg Garrett, "'God Bless White America': Why We Need to Overturn White Racial Mythologies," *Baptist News Global*, January 26, 2021.

39   Baldwin, *The Devil Finds Work,* 524; Eliza Berman, "Moonlight Filmmaker Barry Jenkins on the Bittersweet Feeling of Being a First," *TIME*, February 1, 2017.

40   Baldwin, *The Devil Finds Work,* 524–25.

41   Ibid.

42   Bosley Crowther, "Screen: A Forceful Social Drama; 'The Defiant Ones' Has Debut at Victoria," *New York Times*, September 25, 1958.

43   Baldwin, *The Devil Finds Work,* 525.

44   Ibid., 516.

45   Ibid., 519.

46   Ibid., 520–21.

47   Wesley Morris, "Sidney Poitier Was the Star We Desperately Needed Him to Be," *New York Times*, January 7, 2022.

48   Greg Garrett, "Growing Old with Grace and Kindness: The Life and Lives of Sidney Poitier," *National Catholic Reporter*, January 15, 2021.

49   *If Beale Street Could Talk*, 18–19.

50   Ibid., 33.

51   Ibid., 44, 47, 42.

52   Sharon Waxman, "Inside How 'Moonlight' Director Barry Jenkins and His Cast Turned Personal Pain Into Art," *The Wrap*, November 21, 2016.
53   Elgrably, "James Baldwin, The Art of Fiction No. 78."
54   Ibid.
55   Baldwin, "The New Lost Generation," 659, 660.
56   Baldwin, "The Creative Process," 672.

Baldwin on Faith

1   James Mossman, "Race, Hate, Sex, and Colour: A Conversation with James Baldwin and Colin MacInnes," in *Conversations with James Baldwin*, ed. Fred L. Standley and Louis H. Pratt (Jackson: University Press of Mississippi, 1989), 48.
2   Greg Garrett, "When Great Trees Fall," Wilshire Baptist Church, Dallas, Texas, November 6, 2022.
3   Ayana Mathis, "What the Church Meant for James Baldwin," *New York Times,* December 4, 2020.
4   The British poet William Blake, in his poem "Jerusalem" ("And did those feet in ancient time"), promoted a utopian vision of a world of peace and justice built in England (and, therefore, on Earth); M. S. Handler, "James Baldwin Resists Despair Despite Race 'Drift and Danger,'" *New York Times*, June 3, 1963, 1, 19.
5   John Hall, "James Baldwin Interviewed," in *Conversations with James Baldwin*, 102.
6   Kalamu ya Salaam, "James Baldwin: Looking towards the Eighties," in *Conversations with James Baldwin*, 182.
7   Julius Lester, "James Baldwin—Reflections of a Maverick," in *Conversations with James Baldwin*, 226.
8   Baldwin, *Another Country* (New York: Vintage, 1993 [1962]), 145–46.
9   Robert Park Mills Papers, Box 4 (emphasis in original).
10   Thomas A. Dorsey, "Take My Hand Precious Lord," 1938. Dorsey wrote the song in response to the death of his wife in childbirth. The song was a favorite also of the Rev. Dr. Martin Luther King Jr. Mahalia Jackson sang it at King's funeral in 1968.
11   Proverbs 22:6; James Baldwin, *The Amen Corner* (New York: Vintage, 1998), 26.
12   "I Am Not Your Negro | James Baldwin on the Dick Cavett Show | Netflix," YouTube, July 4, 2020; Baldwin, *No Name in the Street*, 382.

13 Robert Park Mills Papers, Box 3.

14 Buccola, *The Fire Is upon Us*, 166.

15 Danté Stewart, *Shoutin' in the Fire: An American Epistle* (New York: Convergent, 2021), 122–23.

16 Lester, "James Baldwin—Reflections of a Maverick," 226.

17 Charles Kimball, *When Religion Becomes Evil: Five Warning Signs* (New York: HarperOne, 2002), 96, 44.

18 David Leeming, *James Baldwin: A Biography* (New York: Arcade, 2015 [1994]), 56.

19 Ibid., 262.

20 Smith, "Sketches on James Baldwin."

21 Baldwin, *The Fire Next Time*, 296.

22 Paul Tillich, *Systematic Theology,* Vol. 2, *Existence and the Christ* (Chicago: University of Chicago Press, 1975), 44–45.

23 Baldwin, *Another Country*, 49.

24 Ibid., 45.

25 Ibid., 19.

26 Isaiah 41:10 NRSV.

27 Mark 5:36 (author's rendering).

28 Baldwin, *The Fire Next Time*, 291; James Baldwin, *One Day When I Was Lost* (New York: Vintage, 2007 [1972]), 115.

29 Baldwin, *Go Tell It on the Mountain* (New York: Everyman's Library, 2016 [1953]), 10–11.

30 Baldwin, *One Day When I Was Lost*, 191.

31 Baldwin, *The Fire Next Time*, 296.

32 Ibid., 299.

33 Robert Park Mills Papers, Box 3.

34 Mathis, "What the Church Meant for James Baldwin."

35 Baldwin, *No Name in the Street*, 382–83.

36 James H. Cone, *The Cross and the Lynching Tree* (Maryknoll, NY: Orbis Books, 2011), xv.

37 Anthony Reddie, *Introducing James H. Cone: A Personal Exploration* (London: SCM, 2022), 16.

38 "This Far by Faith," PBS.org.

39 Baldwin, *One Day When I Was Lost*, 160–64.

40 Baldwin, *The Fire Next Time*, 309.

41 Jemar Tisby, *The Color of Compromise: The Truth about the American Church's Complicity in Racism* (Grand Rapids: Zondervan, 2022), 66.

42 Ibid., 143.

43 Brian Seage, sermon, Diocese of Mississippi Clergy Conference, Meridian, Mississippi, October 19, 2022.

44 Ralph West, "Commentary: Where I Stand on the Statement by SBC Seminary Presidents," BaptistStandard.com, December 16, 2020.

45 Baldwin, *The Fire Next Time*, 309–10.

46 Ibid., 305.

47 John 13:34 NRSV.

48 Baldwin, *If Beale Street Could Talk* (New York: Vintage, 2006), 25–26.

49 Baldwin, *The Fire Next Time*, 308.

50 Ibid., 327.

51 Ibid., 293–94.

52 Baldwin, *No Name in the Street*, 390–91.

53 Mossman, "Race, Hate, Sex, and Colour," 48.

54 Presiding Bishop Michael Curry, Twitter, July 11, 2017.

55 Hebrews 11:11 KJV.

56 Baldwin, *The Evidence of Things Not Seen* (New York: Owl, 1985), 121.

57 Ibid., 123.

58 Ibid., 122.

Baldwin on Race

1 Dating this Cavett appearance is challenging. In *I Am Not Your Negro*, this clip runs with a caption identifying it as coming from 1968, as does the accompanying book from Vintage. The *Cavett Show* identifies it on YouTube as having aired on May 16, 1969. It is possible that the show originally aired in 1968 and was rebroadcast in 1969. I have chosen to go with the *Cavett Show*'s dating.

2 *The Dick Cavett Show*, May 16, 1969.

3 Baldwin, *No Name in the Street*, 430.

4 Baldwin's script was a source for Spike Lee's *Malcolm X* (1992); because of the extent to which he rewrote and revised Baldwin's script, the Baldwin family asked to have James Baldwin's name removed from the film's credits; ibid., 431.

5 Barbara Fields, "Ideology and Race in American History," in *Region, Race, and Reconstruction: Essays in Honor of C. Vann Woodward*, ed. J. Morgan Kousser and James M. McPherson (New York: Oxford University Press, 1982), 144.

6   Reggie Williams, "Black Paris with Dr. Reggie Williams," The American Church in Paris, May 19, 2022.

7   Kelly Brown Douglas, *Resurrection Hope: A Future Where Black Lives Matter* (Maryknoll, NY: Orbis Books, 2021), 3.

8   Ibram X. Kendi, *Stamped from the Beginning: The Definitive History of Racist Ideas in America* (New York: Nation, 2016), 29.

9   David Olusoga, *Black and British: A Forgotten History* (London: Picador, 2021).

10   Baldwin, *No Name in the Street*, 432.

11   Baldwin, *The Fire Next Time*, 291.

12   Baldwin, *No Name in the Street*, 432.

13   Elgrably, "James Baldwin, The Art of Fiction No. 78."

14   "James Baldwin Discusses His Book, 'Nobody Knows My Name: More Notes of a Native Son,'" Studs Terkel Radio Archive, July 15, 1961, Studsterkel.wfmt.com.

15   Baldwin, "The Negro and the American Promise," 1963, Thirteen.org.

16   Salaam, "James Baldwin: Looking towards the Eighties," 180.

17   Baldwin, *No Name in the Street*, 452.

18   Baldwin, *The Fire Next Time*, 302.

19   Baldwin, "The Negro and the American Promise," 1963.

20   Baldwin, *Go Tell It on the Mountain*, 36–37.

21   Helen Brown Norden, *Vanity Fair*, August 1934; Baldwin, *Go Tell It on the Mountain*, 37.

22   Baldwin, "Has the American Dream Been Achieved at the Expense of the American Negro?," Cambridge Union, Cambridge England, February 18, 1965, YouTube.com.

23   Baldwin, *The Devil Finds Work*, 500.

24   Ibid., 511.

25   For a recent study of Hollywood films and the myths and messages embedded in them, please see my *A Long, Long Way: Hollywood's Unfinished Journey from Racism to Reconciliation* (New York: Oxford University Press, 2020).

26   Baldwin, *The Devil Finds Work*, 525.

27   Greg Garrett, "Dealing with the Truth: An Interview with Sarah Churchwell on Gone with the Wind, the Lost Cause and Donald Trump," *Baptist News Global*, July 28, 2022.

28   Tyler Stovall, *White Freedom: The Racial History of an Idea* (Princeton, NJ: Princeton University Press, 2021), 8.

29   Baldwin, *The Fire Next Time*, 294.
30   Baldwin, *Blues for Mister Charlie* (New York: Vintage, 1995 [1964]), xiv.
31   Baldwin, *The Evidence of Things Not Seen*, 42.
32   Baldwin, *The Fire Next Time*, 292–93.
33   Ibid., 292.
34   Baldwin, *The Cross of Redemption: Uncollected Writings*, ed. Randall Kenan (New York: Vintage, 2011), 184.
35   Baldwin, *Another Country*, 35.
36   Ibid., 133–34.
37   In addition to multiple press accounts and Baldwin's own writing about the meeting, Michael Eric Dyson has written an entire book exploring the event and its aftermath. See Dyson, *What Truth Sounds Like*.
38   Larry Tye, "Tough Talk: Robert Kennedy and the Civil Rights Movement," HistoryNet.com, October 13, 2016.
39   Mark Whitaker, "Speaking Truth to Power—From James Baldwin to Colin Kaepernick," *Washington Post*, June 15, 2018.
40   Sean Illing, "What a 1963 RFK–James Baldwin Meeting Teaches Us about Race in Trump's America," Vox.com, July 28, 2018.
41   John F. Kennedy, "Televised Address to the Nation on Civil Rights," Jfklibrary.org, June 11, 1963.
42   Ibid.
43   Samuel L. Perry and Philip S. Gorski, "With the Buffalo Massacre, White Christian Nationalism Strikes Again," *Washington Post*, May 20, 2022; "Ahead of Anniversary of 1/6 Insurrection, Republicans Remain Entangled in the Big Lie, QAnon, and Temptations toward Political Violence," PRRI.org, January 4, 2022.
44   Baldwin, "Has the American Dream Been Achieved at the Expense of the American Negro?"
45   Cep Dergisi, "James Baldwin Breaks His Silence," in *Conversations with James Baldwin*, 61.
46   See Baldwin, *One Day When I Was Lost*, 262.
47   Baldwin, "The Price May Be Too High," *New York Times*, February 2, 1969.
48   Jemar Tisby, "Is the American Church Inherently Racist?," *New York Times*, August 18, 2020.
49   Reggie Williams, "Black Paris with Dr. Reggie Williams," The American Church in Paris, May 19, 2022.
50   John Mulaney, *Kid Gorgeous at Radio City*, Netflix.com, initially aired May 1, 2018.

51   Baldwin, *No Name in the Street*, 433.
52   Baldwin, "Stranger in the Village," in *Notes of a Native Son*, 124.
53   Ibid., 128–29.
54   Nat Hentoff, "'It's Terrifying,' James Baldwin: The Price of Fame," in *Conversations with James Baldwin*, 36.
55   John Hall, "James Baldwin Interviewed," in *Conversations with James Baldwin*, 100.
56   Baldwin, *The Fire Next Time*, 342.
57   Ibid., 333.
58   Baldwin, *No Name in the Street*, 426.
59   Robert Park Mills Papers, Box 2.
60   Baldwin, *No Name in the Street*, 427–28.
61   Baldwin, *The Evidence of Things Not Seen*, 122.
62   Anthony Reddie, Facebook.com, November 13, 2022.
63   2 Corinthians 5:18 NRSV.
64   Baldwin, *No Name in the Street*, 406.
65   Baldwin, "The Price of the Ticket," in *James Baldwin: Collected Essays*, 839.
66   Baldwin, "The Negro and the American Promise."
67   Baldwin, *The Evidence of Things Not Seen*, 124–25.
68   Baldwin, *The Fire Next Time*, 338.

Baldwin on Justice

1   Baldwin, *Notes of a Native Son*, 64–65.
2   Baldwin, *The Fire Next Time*, 298.
3   Ibid., 326.
4   Baldwin, *Go Tell It on the Mountain*, 70–71.
5   Baldwin, *The Amen Corner*, 75.
6   Baldwin, *Blues for Mister Charlie*, 77.
7   Ibid., xv.
8   Ecclesiastes 7:20 KJV.
9   Genesis 18:22–26 KJV.
10   *The Oxford Companion to the Bible*, ed. Bruce M. Metzger and Michael D. Coogan (New York: Oxford, 1993), 405.
11   Jeremiah 22:1–5 NRSV.
12   John M. Bracke, "Justice in the Book of Jeremiah," *Word & World* 22, no. 4 (2002): 388.
13   Jeremiah 5:1 NRSV.

14 Baldwin, *The Evidence of Things Not Seen*, 31.

15 Hulitt Gloer, text message, September 2, 2022; Micah 6:8 NRSV.

16 Baldwin, *No Name in the Street*, 374, 386.

17 Jeremiah 7:32–34 NRSV.

18 Matthew 22:13 et al.

19 As in Deuteronomy 28:36–37.

20 Martin Luther King Jr., "Remaining Awake through a Great Revolution," sermon, Washington National Cathedral, March 31, 1968.

21 Baldwin, *Blues for Mister Charlie*, 38.

22 Baldwin, "Equal in Paris," in *Notes of a Native Son*, 103.

23 Ibid., 105–6.

24 Ibid., 109.

25 Ibid., 110–11.

26 Ibid., 115–16.

27 See *Go Tell It on the Mountain*, 180.

28 Ibid., 181.

29 Ibid., 182–83.

30 Ibid., 185.

31 Ibid.

32 Ibid., 186.

33 Hugh Hebert, "James Baldwin's Much Anticipated New Novel—Archive," *The Guardian*, June 18, 2016.

34 Erin Blakemore, "How the Assassination of Medgar Evers Galvanized the Civil Rights Movement," *National Geographic*, June 12, 2020.

35 Baldwin, *No Name in the Street*, 414.

36 Ibid., 416.

37 Ibid., 417.

38 Ibid., 418.

39 Ibid., 419.

40 Ibid., 421.

41 Ibid., 112.

42 Ibid., 422.

43 Ibid., 441.

44 C. Gerald Fraser, "3-Minute Hearing Frees Prisoner in Death Case," *New York Times*, April 5, 1974.

45 Eliza Berman, "Barry Jenkins Wants You to Read James Baldwin," *TIME*, December 6, 2018.

46 *If Beale Street Could Talk*, 185.

47   Ibid., 4.

48   Ibid., 191–92.

49   Dylan Kroll, "Andrew Young: How Atlanta Became the 'City Too Busy to Hate,'" Yahoo Finance, August 24, 2022.

50   Baldwin, *The Evidence of Things Not Seen*, 38.

51   "Fatal Police Shootings of Unarmed Black People in US More Than 3 Times as High as in Whites," BMJ.com, October 27, 2020.

52   "Rate of Fatal Police Shootings in the United States from 2015 to October 2022, by Ethnicity," Statista.com, November 1, 2022.

53   Baldwin, *The Evidence of Things Not Seen*, 43.

54   Berman, "Barry Jenkins Wants You to Read James Baldwin."

55   Baldwin, *Blues for Mister Charlie*, xiv.

56   James Baldwin Papers, MG 936, Box 32, Folder 6, Schomburg Center for Research in Black Culture, New York.

57   Edward E. Baptist, *The Half Has Never Been Told* (New York: Basic Books, 2014), 35.

58   Baldwin, *The Fire Next Time*, 347.

59   See Baldwin, *Blues for Mister Charlie*, 42.

60   Goldstein, "'Go the Way Your Blood Beats,'" 73.

61   Baldwin, *No Name in the Street*, 437.

62   Baldwin, "Faulkner and Desegregation," in *Nobody Knows My Name*, 209.

63   Studs Terkel, "An Interview with James Baldwin," in *James Baldwin: The Last Interview and Other Conversations*, 17.

64   Dagmawi Woubshet, "How James Baldwin's Writings about Love Evolved," *The Atlantic*, January 9, 2019.

65   Martin Luther King Jr., "Loving Your Enemies," in *Strength to Love* (Boston: Beacon, 1981), 47.

66   Baldwin, "The News from All the Northern Cities Is, to Understate It, Grim," *New York Times*, April 5, 1978.

67   See Amos 5:24.

68   See Isaiah 11:6 and 65:25. Although often paraphrased as "lion" and lamb, these verses actually specify a wolf, not a lion, who will lie down with a lamb.

Baldwin on Identity

1   Smith, "Sketches on James Baldwin."

2   Baldwin, "Notes for a Hypothetical Novel: An Address," in *Nobody Knows My Name*, 229–30.

3   Baldwin, "Encounters on the Seine," in *Notes of a Native Son*, 86–87.
4   W. E. B. Du Bois, "Strivings of the Negro People," *Atlantic Monthly*, August 1897.
5   Baldwin, "Encounters on the Seine," 87.
6   Elgrably, "James Baldwin, The Art of Fiction No. 78."
7   Terkel, "An Interview with James Baldwin," 4–7.
8   Ibid., 6.
9   Baldwin, *The Fire Next Time*, 291.
10 Baldwin, *One Day When I Was Lost*, 42–44.
11 Baldwin, *Blues for Mister Charlie*, 117.
12 Ibid., 120.
13 Baldwin, *The Evidence of Things Not Seen*, 20–21.
14 Elgrably, "James Baldwin, The Art of Fiction No. 78."
15 Baldwin, "A Fly in Buttermilk," in *Nobody Knows My Name*, 194.
16 Elgrably, "James Baldwin, The Art of Fiction No. 78."
17 Baldwin, "In Search of a Majority," in *Nobody Knows My Name*, 218.
18 Baldwin, "The Harlem Ghetto," in *Notes of a Native Son*, 48.
19 Elgrably, "James Baldwin, The Art of Fiction No. 78."
20 Charlie Wachtel, David Rabinowitz, Kevin Willmott, and Spike Lee, *BlacKkKlansman*, November 16, 2016 draft, revised, 16–17. https://imsdb.com/scripts/BlacKkKlansman.html.
21 Malcolm X and Alex Haley, *The Autobiography of Malcolm X* (New York: Random House, 1992 [1965]), 65.
22 Baldwin, *One Day When I Was Lost*, 136–37.
23 Charlie Wachtel et al., *BlacKkKlansman*, 17.
24 Baldwin, *No Name in the Street*, 471.
25 Baldwin, *The Fire Next Time*, 294.
26 Baldwin speaking to Kenneth B. Clark, "A Conversation with James Baldwin," in *Conversations with James Baldwin*, 45.
27 Baldwin, *One Day When I Was Lost*, 136.
28 Baldwin, "Nothing Personal," in *James Baldwin: Collected Essays*, 694–95.
29 Terkel, "An Interview with James Baldwin," 20.
30 Baldwin, "Lockridge: The American Myth," in *James Baldwin: Collected Essays*, 589.
31 Baldwin, "The New Lost Generation," 667.
32 Baldwin, *Another Country*, 253–54.
33 Baldwin, *The Amen Corner*, 52–53.
34 Baldwin, "Preservation of Innocence," in *James Baldwin: Collected Essays*, 600.

35   Elgrably, "James Baldwin, The Art of Fiction No. 78."
36   Baldwin, "In Search of a Majority," 220.
37   Goldstein, "'Go the Way Your Blood Beats,'" 61.
38   Ibid., 59, 63.
39   Baldwin, *The Amen Corner*, 57; this is Sister Boxer's paraphrase of 1 John 4:20.
40   Baldwin, *Another Country*, 342–43.
41   Baldwin, *If Beale Street Could Talk*, 190.
42   Baldwin, *Just above My Head* (New York: Delta, 1979), 4.
43   James Baldwin Papers, MG 936, Box 35, Folder 1.
44   *If Beale Street Could Talk*, 44, 49.
45   Goldstein, "'Go the Way Your Blood Beats,'" 70–71.
46   Ibid., 73.
47   Baldwin, "Notes for a Hypothetical Novel," 229.

Journey's End, New Beginnings

1   Goldstein, "'Go the Way Your Blood Beats,'" 74.
2   Baldwin, *The Amen Corner*, 78.

9 781626 985391